Anonymous

The Stranger's illustrated Pocket Guide to Philadelphia

Embracing a Description of the principal Objects of Interest in and around the City

Anonymous

The Stranger's illustrated Pocket Guide to Philadelphia
Embracing a Description of the principal Objects of Interest in and around the City

ISBN/EAN: 9783337193812

Printed in Europe, USA, Canada, Australia, Japan

Cover: Foto ©Lupo / pixelio.de

More available books at **www.hansebooks.com**

THE

STRANGER'S ILLUSTRATED

POCKET GUIDE

TO

PHILADELPHIA

EMBRACING

A DESCRIPTION OF THE PRINCIPAL OBJECTS
OF INTEREST IN AND AROUND THE CITY,
WITH DIRECTIONS HOW TO REACH THEM.

INCLUDING

THE GROUNDS AND BUILDINGS OF THE
CENTENNIAL EXHIBITION.

PHILADELPHIA:
J. B. LIPPINCOTT & CO.
1876.

TO VISITORS.

Persons unacquainted with the city should, at the outset, become familiar with the system of numbering the houses. On the streets running west from the Delaware River, the houses are divided into *squares* or *blocks*, by cross-streets, named consecutively, Front, Second, Third, Fourth, etc., and the commencement of each square or block commences also a new hundred in the numbering. For instance, at Second Street the numbering commences with 200, at Third Street with 300, at Fourth Street with 400, etc.

The streets running north and south are also divided into squares in the same manner, Market Street being the dividing line between north and south. The following streets commence new squares, north and south of Market Street respectively:

NO.	NORTH.	NO.	SOUTH.
1	Market.	1	Market.
100	Arch.	100	Chestnut.
200	Race.	200	Walnut.
300	Vine.	300	Spruce.
400	Callowhill.	400	Pine.
500	Buttonwood.	500	Lombard.
600	Green.	600	South.
700	Fairmount Avenue.	700	Bainbridge.
800	Brown.	800	Catharine.
900	Poplar.	900	Christian.
1200	Girard Avenue.	1000	Carpenter.
1300	Thompson.	1100	Washington.
1400	Master.	1200	Federal.
1500	Jefferson.	1300	Wharton.
1600	Oxford.	1400	Reed.
1700	Columbia Avenue.	1500	Dickinson.
1800	Montgomery Avenue.	1600	Tasker.
1900	Berks.	1700	Morris.
2000	Norris.	1800	Moore.
2100	Diamond.	1900	Mifflin.
2200	Susquehanna Avenue.	2000	McKean.
2300	Dauphin.	2100	Snyder.
2400	York.	2200	Jackson.
2500	Cumberland.	2300	Wolf.
2600	Huntingdon.	2400	Ritner.
2700	Lehigh Avenue.	2500	Porter.
2800	Somerset.	2600	Shunk.
2900	Cambria.	2700	Oregon Avenue.
3000	Indiana.	2800	Johnson.
3100	Clearfield.	2900	Bigler.
3200	Allegheny Avenue.	3000	Pollock.
		3100	Packer.
		3200	Curtin.

[Copyright, 1876.]

PREFACE.

THE design of this little work, as stated in its title, is to afford a convenient guide to the principal objects of interest in and around Philadelphia, with directions as to the most available methods by which the different points can be reached.

To render the work easy of reference, an alphabetical arrangement of *subjects* or *general heads* has been adopted, under which may be found the special subjects, also arranged in alphabetical order.

It is believed that the work leaves little to be desired in the way of a convenient guide to the city and surroundings.

THE STRANGER'S ILLUSTRATED GUIDE TO PHILADELPHIA.

ACADEMY OF FINE ARTS.

The new building of the **Pennsylvania Academy of Fine Arts**, recently opened, is situated at the southwest corner of Broad and Cherry Streets, having a front on Broad Street of one hundred feet, with a depth on Cherry Street of two hundred and sixty feet. The structure is fireproof, of brick and stone, in the Venetian style of architecture. Commodious class- and lecture-rooms furnish ample accommodations to students, to whom gratuitous instruction is given in the various branches of art, and spacious galleries lighted from the ceilings afford excellent opportunities for exhibiting to the best advantage the art treasures of the Academy. Of the many attractive institutions of Philadelphia, few better repay a visit than this. To visitors it is accessible from the northern section of the city by the cars on Thirteenth Street and on Seventeenth Street, passing near the Academy at Cherry or Arch Street; from the west by the Race Street cars, passing at Broad Street a few doors distant; by the Arch Street cars, passing at Broad Street within a few feet of the door; and by the Market Street cars, stopping at Broad Street. From the south the Academy is reached by the cars on Fifteenth and Sixteenth Streets, stopping at Arch or Cherry Street; and from the east by the cars on Arch Street, Market Street, and Vine Street, stopping at Broad Street. Other lines of cars connecting with these by *exchange tickets* (price, nine cents) render the Academy easily accessible from all sections.

ACADEMY OF NATURAL SCIENCES.

The **Academy of Natural Sciences of Philadelphia**, situated at Nineteenth and Race Streets, is among the most interesting of the institutions of the city. It was founded in 1812, by a few gentlemen who met together at stated times for the purpose of exchanging views upon scientific subjects; and from that small beginning has since arisen one of the grandest scientific institutions in the country. For many years prior to 1876 the Academy was located at Broad and Sansom Streets, occupying the building now known as the Hotel Lafayette; but its quarters then becoming too contracted for the large and rapidly-increasing collections, the present fine structure was erected. The following are among the contents of the museum; natural objects, two hundred and fifty thousand specimens, representing every department of zoology, geology, and botany; palæontological specimens, sixty thousand; mineralogical specimens, five thousand; species of plants, ten thousand; species of insects, twenty-five thousand; specimens of shells, one hundred thousand, the collection being only excelled by that of the British Museum; birds, thirty-one thousand, probably unequaled by any collection in Europe; reptiles, eight hundred species; fishes, eleven hundred species; mammals, one thousand specimens, together with two hundred and seventy-one skeletons, three hundred and forty-six crania, and twelve hundred human crania of various races. The Academy is accessible from the eastern section of the city by the Vine Street cars and by the Arch Street cars, both passing at Nineteenth Street, one square distant; from the north by the Seventeenth Street cars, passing at Race Street, two squares distant; from the west by the Race Street cars, which pass the door, and the Arch Street cars, which pass one square distant; and from the south by the Nineteenth Street cars, which pass the building. Other lines from almost all sections of the city *exchange* with the foregoing. The Academy is open to visitors daily, except on Saturdays and Sundays. Admission 25 cents; children 10 cents.

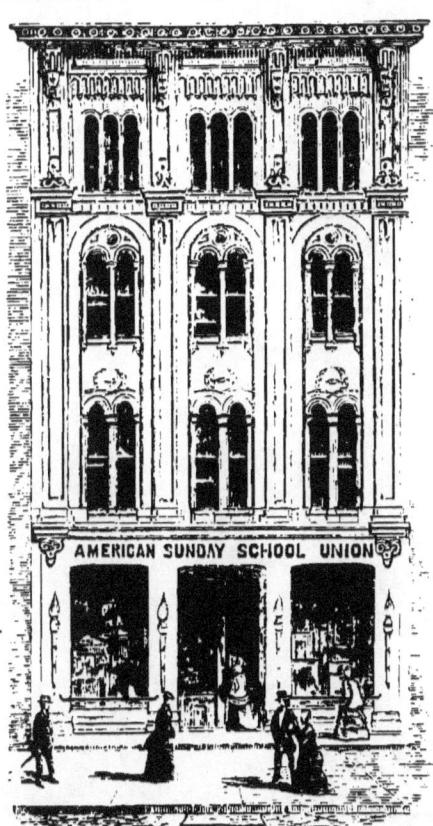

AMERICAN SUNDAY-SCHOOL UNION.

AMERICAN SUNDAY-SCHOOL UNION.

The central office of the **American Sunday-school Union** is situated at 1122 Chestnut Street. The building is granite, in the Norman-Gothic style. The Sunday-school Union was founded in 1817, and instituted under the present name in 1824; since which time it has been steadily at work in its appointed mission of instructing and elevating the masses of the people in destitute localities through the medium of Sunday-schools.

NEW ACADEMY OF NATURAL SCIENCES.

AMUSEMENTS AND AUDIENCE HALLS.

The **Academy of Music**—foremost among our places of amusement in general importance—is situated on the southwest corner of Broad and Locust Streets. Its architecture is of the Italian Byzantine School, such as is frequently seen in the northern parts of Italy. The auditorium is one hundred and two feet long, ninety feet wide, and seventy feet high, and will seat twenty-nine hundred persons besides providing standing room for six hundred more. Its arrangements both for seeing and hearing are excellent, its acoustic properties being extolled by all who have appeared on its stage. All the appointments of the building are on a scale commensurate with the immense size of the auditorium, and go to make up one of the most complete and magnificent opera-houses in the world. Persons visiting the Academy by means of the passenger railways running down Thirteenth Street or up Fifteenth Street, leave the cars at Locust Street. The cars running eastward on Spruce Street or westward on Walnut Street also pass (at Broad Street) within a short distance of the Academy. Other railway lines connecting with these routes by means of *exchange tickets* (price nine cents) render the Academy easily accessible from all parts of the city.

Amateur Drawing-Room is situated on Seventeenth Street, above Chestnut. Occasional dramatic performances and readings are given here, principally by amateurs. Passenger cars going southward, on Seventeenth Street, pass the door, and the cars on Chestnut, Market, and Walnut Streets pass at Seventeenth Street, very near the Drawing-Room.

Arch Street Opera-House (Simmons and Slocum's Minstrels) is situated on Arch Street, above Tenth, and is reached by the cars on Arch Street, which pass the door. The cars passing down Tenth Street and the Ridge Avenue cars on their downward route also pass the building at Tenth and Arch Streets.

Arch Street Theatre, located on Arch Street, above Sixth, is one of the standard places of amusement in the city. Its interior arrangements are excellent. The auditorium will seat eighteen hundred persons, and the dimensions of its stage, sixty-seven feet square by thirty feet high, give ample room for representations. The Fifth and Sixth Street cars and the Union line pass at Arch Street, near the theatre, and the Arch Street and Ridge Avenue lines pass the door.

Assembly Buildings, situated at the southwest corner of Tenth and Chestnut Streets (entrance on Tenth Street), is used for balls, concerts, panoramas, etc. Accessible from the western portion of the city by the Chestnut and Market Street cars (stopping at Tenth Street), from the north by the Tenth Street cars, and from the south by the Eleventh Street cars (stopping at Eleventh and Chestnut Streets) and the Union line, stopping at Ninth and Chestnut Streets.

Chestnut Street Theatre, situated on the north side of Chestnut Street, above Twelfth, is neatly built, and is considered architecturally among the most attractive theatres in the city. Cars passing down Chestnut Street convey visitors to the door. The theatre is accessible

from the northern part of the city by the cars on **Twelfth** and **Thirteenth** Streets, from the southern section by the cars on **Eleventh** Street, from the east by the cars on Walnut Street, and from both the east and west by the cars on Market street.

THE **Colosseum** is situated on the southeast corner of Broad and Locust Streets, opposite the Academy of Music, and was constructed for the purpose of exhibiting the painting of "Paris by Night," and other similar works. It is a cylindrical structure about one hundred and thirty feet in diameter, the wall rising to the height of about eighty feet, and surmounted by a tower one hundred and sixty-six feet from the level of the street. Accessible from the north by the Thirteenth Street cars (stopping at Locust Street), from the east by the Walnut Street cars (stopping at Broad Street), from the south by the Fifteenth Street cars (stopping at Locust Street), and from the west by the Chestnut Street and Spruce Street cars, stopping at Broad Street.

Concert Hall, a popular audience-room, on Chestnut Street, above Twelfth, with a seating capacity of about twelve hundred. (For means of access, see CHESTNUT STREET THEATRE.)

Concordia Hall, on Callowhill Street, above Fourth Street, is used as a German Theatre, Opera-House, and Concert-Room. Accessible by cars down Second, Fourth, and Sixth Streets, and up Third and Fifth Streets. The Callowhill Street cars also pass the Hall going in both directions.

Eleventh Street Opera-House (Carncross and Dixey's Minstrels), on Eleventh Street, above Chestnut, is a well-known and popular establishment. The cars from the southern section of the city pass the door on Eleventh Street, and the Market Street and Chestnut Street lines run within a half-square.

Forrest Mansion Garden, at the residence of the late Edwin Forrest, corner of Broad and Master Streets. Accessible from the south by the cars on Fifteenth Street and on Sixteenth Street, stopping at Master; from the north by the cars on Seventeenth and Thirteenth Streets, also stopping at Master; and from the eastern and western sections of the city by the railway lines exchanging with these routes.

Fox's American Theatre (Varieties), on Chestnut Street, between Tenth and Eleventh, is among the most popular places of amusement in the city. Cars on Chestnut Street pass the door. Cars on Eleventh Street from the southern section of the city pass (at Eleventh and Chestnut Streets) within a half-square, and cars from the north down Tenth bring visitors to Tenth and Chestnut Streets, only a few doors from the theatre. The Market Street cars also run within a square of the place—visitors by this route leaving the cars at either Tenth and Market or Eleventh and Market Streets.

Grand Central Variety Theatre, on Walnut Street, above Eighth Street, is accessible by the cars of the Union line from the northern section of the city, which pass, at Seventh and Walnut Streets, within a square of the theatre. The same line from the southern section of the city takes visitors to Ninth and Walnut Streets, within a few doors

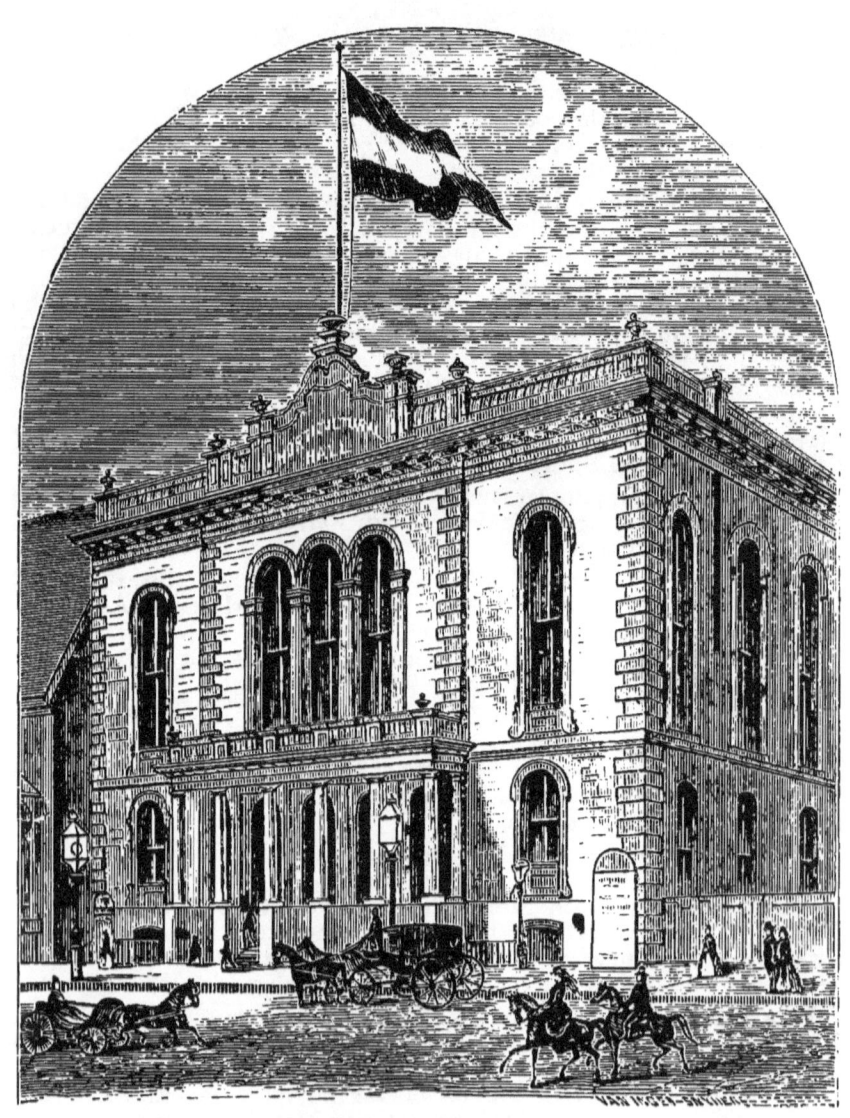

HORTICULTURAL HALL.

of the place, and the cars from the same section up Eighth Street pass near the door at Walnut Street. Visitors from the west by the Chestnut Street and Spruce Street lines leave the cars at Eighth Street. The Walnut Street cars from the east pass the door, and *alternate cars* on the Fourth and Eighth Streets and Green Street and Fairmount Avenue lines pass up Walnut Street from Fourth to Eighth, leaving visitors at Eighth and Walnut Streets.

Handel and Haydn Hall. The hall of the Handel and Haydn Society, situated at the northeast corner of Eighth and Spring Garden Streets, is accessible from the south by the cars on Eighth Street, and by the cars of the Union line passing up Ninth to Spring Garden; from the north and northwest by the cars of the Union line, of the Green Street line, stopping at Eighth, and of the Sixth Street and the Tenth Street lines, stopping at Spring Garden.

Horticultural Hall. The hall of the Pennsylvania Horticultural Society is situated on the west side of Broad Street, above Spruce, adjoining the Academy of Music. It is an imposing brick structure, with sandstone front. Besides the exhibitions of the Society it is frequently used for lectures, concerts, and other entertainments. Accessible from the north by the Thirteenth Street cars (stopping at Locust or Spruce Street); from the south by the Fifteenth Street cars (stopping also at Locust or Spruce Street); from the east by the Walnut Street line (stopping at Broad); and from the west by the Spruce Street line, stopping also at Broad. Other lines of cars exchanging with these lines render the hall easily accessible from all sections of the city.

Kiralfys' Alhambra, situated on Broad Street, between Spruce and Locust, nearly opposite the Academy of Music, is designed for musical and dramatic performances, under the direction of the Kiralfy Brothers. It contains seating capacity for about one thousand persons. Connected with the theatre is a garden handsomely laid out and ornamented. This theatre is reached from the north by the Thirteenth Street cars, stopping at Locust or Spruce Street; from the east by the cars on Walnut and Pine Streets (both passing at Broad Street, within two squares of the place); from the south by the cars on Fifteenth Street (stopping at Spruce or at Locust Street); and from the west by the cars on Spruce Street, stopping at Broad.

Musical Fund Hall. The hall of the Musical Fund Society is situated on Locust Street, above Eighth Street. Accessible from the northern section of the city by the cars of the Union line, stopping at Locust Street; from the south by the cars of the same line, stopping at Ninth and Locust Streets, and the cars on Eighth Street, stopping at Locust Street; from the west by the cars on Spruce Street, stopping at Eighth Street; and from the east by the cars on Walnut Street. Cars going east on Chestnut Street also pass (at Eighth Street) within about two squares of the hall.

New National Theatre (Varieties), situated at the southwest corner of Tenth and Callowhill Streets, can be reached from the east and west by the Callowhill Street cars; from the north by the Tenth Street cars; from the south by the Eleventh Street cars, which pass (at Eleventh and Callowhill Streets) within one square of the theatre. The Ridge Avenue cars from both directions pass the door.

Walnut Street Theatre, situated on the corner of Ninth and Walnut Streets. Is accessible from the southern section of the city by the cars of the Union line, which pass the building, and the cars on Eighth Street, which pass one square distant; from the west by the cars on Chestnut and Spruce Streets, stopping at Ninth Street, from the north by the cars on Tenth Street, stopping at Tenth and Walnut, and by the cars of the Union line, stopping at Seventh and Walnut Streets. Cars going west on Walnut Street pass the door, and the Walnut Street branch of the Green Street cars conveys visitors to Eighth and Walnut Streets, one square from the theatre.

Wood's Museum, a museum of curiosities with a theatrical department, is situated at the corner of Ninth and Arch Streets. It is accessible from the western portion of the city by the cars on Arch Street, which pass the door; from the northwest by the Ridge Avenue cars, which also pass the building; and from the north by the Tenth Street cars, which (at Tenth and Arch) pass within one square. From the southern section of the city the Union line of cars conveys passengers direct to the Museum, and the cars on Eighth Street pass (at Eighth and Arch) within one square.

Armories. See MILITARY ESTABLISHMENTS.

Asylums. See HOSPITALS AND ASYLUMS.

Athenæum. See LIBRARIES.

BANKS AND SAVINGS INSTITUTIONS.

The banking institutions of Philadelphia are principally within the locality bounded by Arch Street on the north, by Spruce Street on the south, by Second Street on the east, and by Fifth Street on the west. This locality is reached from the northern and northwestern sections of the city by the cars on Second and Fourth Streets; by the cars of the Union line (Market Street branch), which run to Second and Market Streets; by the Ridge Avenue cars, which run to Second and Arch Streets; and by the Green Street cars, which run down Fourth Street. From the western section of the city the locality is reached by the Arch Street cars, the Market Street cars, the Chestnut Street cars, and the Spruce Street cars; and from the south the section is reached by the Third Street cars and the Fifth Street cars. Other lines of cars connecting with the foregoing by *exchange tickets* (price 9 cents) render the locality easily accessible from all directions.

The following are among the principal banking institutions in Philadelphia:

Bank of America, 306 Walnut Street, south side, above Third Street.

Bank of North America, 307 Chestnut Street, north side, above Third Street.

BANKS AND SAVINGS INSTITUTIONS.

Beneficial Saving Fund, southwest corner of Twelfth and Chestnut Streets.

Centennial National Bank, 3126 Market Street, West Philadelphia.

Central National Bank, 109 South Fourth Street, below Chestnut Street.

City National Bank, 32 North Sixth Street, between Market and Arch Streets.

Commercial National Bank, 314 Chestnut Street, south side, above Third Street.

Commonwealth National Bank, on the corner of Fourth and Walnut Streets.

Consolidation National Bank, 331 North Third Street, above Vine Street.

Corn Exchange National Bank, on the corner of Second and Chestnut Streets.

Eighth National Bank, on the corner of Second Street and Girard Avenue.

Farmers' and Mechanics' National Bank, 427 Chestnut Street, opposite the Custom-House.

First National Bank, 313 Chestnut Street, north side, above Third Street.

Girard National Bank, Third Street, between Chestnut and Walnut Streets.

Keystone Bank, 1326 Chestnut Street, on the southwest corner of Chestnut and Juniper Streets.

Manufacturers' National Bank, 27 North Third Street, above Market Street.

Mechanics' National Bank, 22 South Third Street, between Market and Chestnut Streets.

National Bank of Commerce, 209 Chestnut Street, above Second Street.

National Bank of the Northern Liberties, Third and Vine Streets.

National Bank of the Republic, 320 Chestnut Street, south side, below Fourth Street.

National Security Bank, corner of Seventh Street and Girard Avenue.

Northern Savings Fund, Safe Deposit, and Trust Company, Sixth and Spring Garden Streets.

Peoples' Bank, 435 Chestnut Street, on the north side, below Fifth Street.

Penn National Bank, on the corner of Sixth and Vine Streets.

BANKS AND SAVINGS INSTITUTIONS.

Philadelphia National Bank, 423 Chestnut Street, opposite the Custom-House.

Philadelphia Savings Fund Society, corner of Seventh and Walnut Streets.

PHILADELPHIA SAVINGS FUND.

Seventh National Bank, on the corner of Fourth and Market Streets.

Sixth National Bank, on the corner of Second and Pine Streets.

Southwark National Bank, 610 South Second Street, below South Street.

Spring Garden Bank, corner of Ridge Avenue and Spring Garden Street.

Third National Bank, southwest corner of Market Street and Penn Square.

Tradesmen's National Bank, 113 South Third Street, below Chestnut.

Union Banking Company, 310 Chestnut Street, south side, above Third Street.

Union National Bank, on the northeast corner of Third and Arch Streets.

United States Banking Company, corner of Tenth and Chestnut Streets.

LOOKING EAST FROM BELMONT.

West Philadelphia Bank, 3938 Market Street, West Philadelphia.

Western National Bank, 406 and 408 Chestnut Street, above Fourth Street.

Western Saving Fund Society, corner of Tenth and Walnut Streets.

BELMONT.

Belmont, once a fine estate, now included in FAIRMOUNT PARK (q. v.), was celebrated in Revolutionary times as the home of Judge Richard Peters, poet, punster, patriot, and jurist. The "mansion"—now a restaurant—is situated on a fine elevation north by east of George's Hill and nearly west from the Belmont station of the Reading Railroad, from which a beautiful walk through Belmont Glen leads to the "mansion," about half a mile distant. The place is also approached from Forty-fourth Street and Girard Avenue, by way of Belmont Avenue, which leads through the Park.

The view from the piazza of the house is one which can scarcely be surpassed in America. Our engraving, though drawn by one of the first landscape painters in the country, gives but a faint idea of its beauty. It is one of those grand effects of nature and art combined which man must acknowledge his inability to represent adequately on paper.

BELMONT PARK,

A new race-course, on the Bryn Mawr road, about five miles from Market Street Bridge, and near Elm Station, on the Pennsylvania Railroad. The course is one mile in extent, and is fitted up with the usual conveniences of a first-class track, including a grand stand and saloon for ladies and gentlemen.

BLOCKLEY ALMSHOUSE.

The city Almshouse is on the west side of the Schuylkill, nearly opposite the Naval Asylum, and is reached by the Walnut Street cars (Darby branch), which pass the Almshouse at Thirty-seventh Street. The grounds contain one hundred and seventy-nine acres, and the estimated value of the property is about three million dollars. A large portion of the grounds is cultivated, constituting a fine farm. Cars on lines running north and south connect with the Walnut Street line by *exchange tickets* (price nine cents), rendering the institution easily accessible from all parts of the city. The buildings themselves occupy about ten acres, and will accommodate conveniently three thousand inmates.

BOAT CLUBS.

To visitors interested in aquatic sports the Boat Clubs are an attractive feature. The headquarters of these clubs are generally on the Schuylkill River just above the FAIRMOUNT WATER-WORKS. They consist of from fifty to one hundred active members each, and the value of their boating apparatus ranges from fifteen hundred to five thousand

B

18 *BRIDGES.*

dollars. Several of the clubs have attractive boat-houses, ranging in cost from four thousand to eight thousand dollars. The vicinity of the boat-houses is reached by the Fairmount Avenue cars, which pass up Eighth Street, by the cars of the Union line (Fairmount branch), by

BOAT HOUSES ON THE SCHUYLKILL.

the Callowhill Street cars going west, by the Vine Street cars, by the Arch Street cars going west, and by the Pine Street cars (Fairmount branch), all of which have their termini near the Fairmount Water-Works.

BRIDGES.

Chestnut Street Bridge, across the Schuylkill River, is a fine, substantial structure of stone and iron, having an entire length of over fifteen hundred feet. It spans the river by two arches, each about four hundred feet long, resting upon a middle pier. The cars of the Chestnut and Walnut Street Railroad pass over this bridge, in both directions, and the Pine Street cars (Fairmount branch) pass at Twenty-third and Chestnut Streets, within two squares of the bridge; the Market Street cars also pass, one square distant, at the Schuylkill River. Visitors can reach the bridge from the northern and southern sections of the city, by means of *exchange tickets* (price nine cents), procurable from the conductors of the roads running north and south, and good for the Walnut Street or Market Street roads.

Columbia Bridge, originally built for the use of the Columbia Railroad, is a wooden structure within the limits of Fairmount Park,

CHESTNUT STREET BRIDGE.

BRIDGES.

near Belmont. The track of the Reading Railroad occupies one side of the bridge—a carriage-way the other. It is over one thousand feet long. The Park trains on the Reading Railroad stop near the bridge, and the steamers on the Schuylkill have landings in the vicinity. The surrounding scenery is very agreeable.

Connecting Railroad Bridge, a massive structure across the Schuylkill, on the line of the Pennsylvania Railroad, over which pass the West Philadelphia trains to and from New York. It is situated within the boundaries of Fairmount Park, just above Girard Avenue Bridge, and is reached from the city by the Girard Avenue cars, and by the cars of lines running north and south, connecting by *exchange tickets* (price nine cents) with the Girard Avenue line; the cars of the Union line (Fairmount branch) also convey passengers to Twenty-ninth and Brown Streets, the east entrance to Fairmount Park, a short distance from the bridge.

Fairmount Bridge, across the Schuylkill River, below the Fairmount Water-Works, is a new and elegant "double deck" iron truss

FALLS RAILROAD BRIDGE.

bridge which has just taken the place of the once celebrated Wire Bridge. This new bridge is one of the most elaborate structures of its kind in this country. It was designed by J. H. Linville, and erected by the

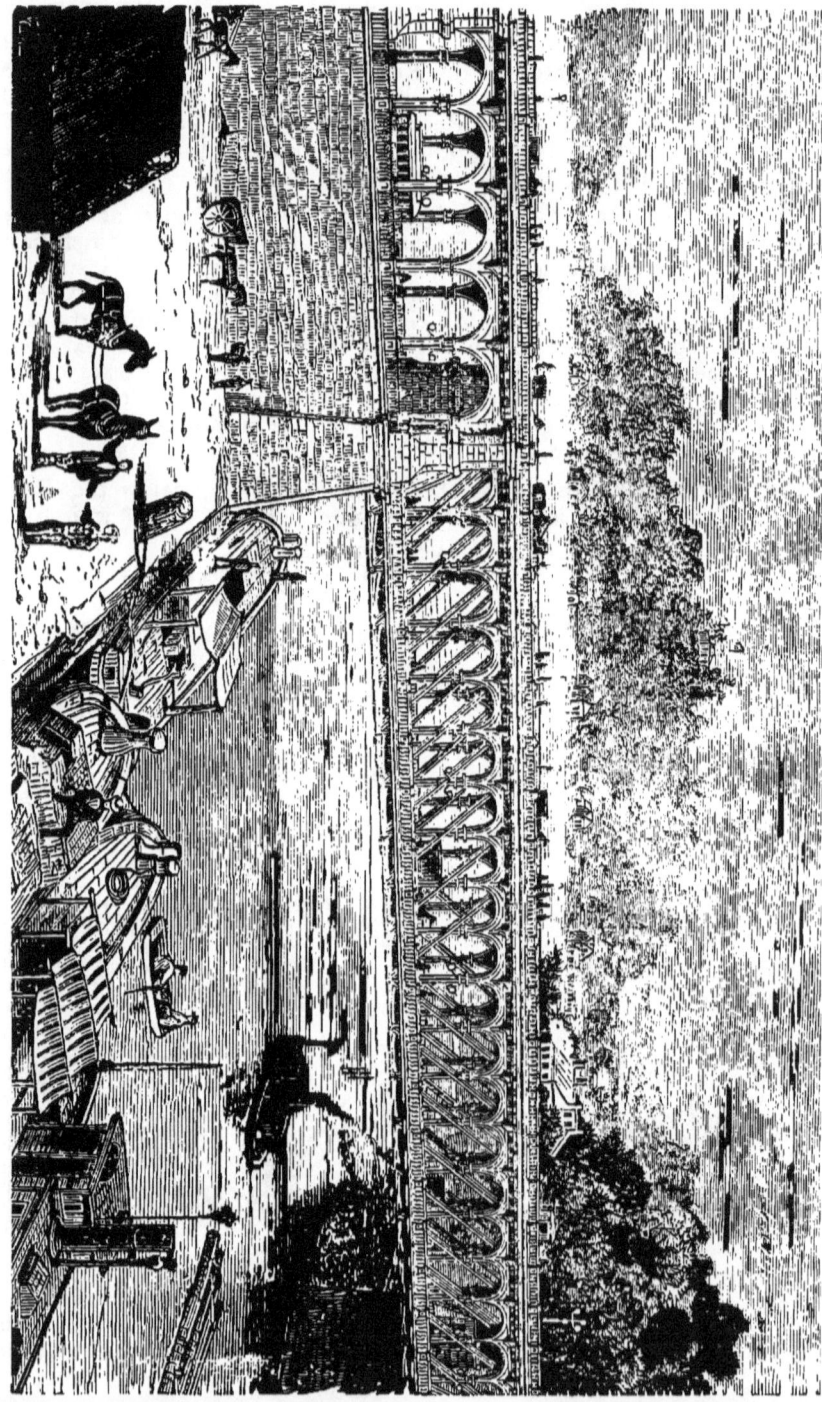

Keystone Bridge Company. The total length of the superstructure is twelve hundred and seventy-four feet, the main span over the river being three hundred and fifty feet. The bridge has an upper and lower roadway and sidewalks, and is forty-eight feet in width; the upper roadway is elevated thirty-two feet above Callowhill Street, and connects Spring Garden Street on the east with Bridge Street on the west. The lower roadway connects Callowhill Street with Haverford Street. Fairmount Bridge may be reached by the cars on Callowhill Street, by the Vine Street cars, by the Arch Street cars going west, and by the Fairmount branch of the Pine Street cars. The cars of the Union line (Fairmount branch) also pass up Spring Garden Street to the immediate vicinity of the bridge.

Falls Railroad Bridge is a massive stone structure, across the Schuylkill River, on the line of the Port Richmond branch of the Reading Railroad, just above the northern boundary of Laurel Hill Cemetery. It is about six hundred feet in length, and has five piers, supporting arches of about eighty feet span. The bridge is used principally by the coal trains of the Reading Railroad, running to Port Richmond. Passenger trains of this road from the depot at Broad and Callowhill Streets cross the Schuylkill River by the COLUMBIA BRIDGE, (q. v.), and, passing up the west bank of the river, make a stop in the immediate vicinity of the Falls Bridge. The Ridge Avenue cars pass the bridge on the east.

Falls of Schuylkill Bridge, a wooden structure, for general travel across the Schuylkill River, at the Falls Village, is in the direct carriage-route between West Fairmount Park and the Wissahickon. As a specimen of architecture, it possesses no unusual merit.

Girard Avenue Bridge, an elegant iron structure, over the Schuylkill River, connecting the East and West Parks. This bridge was opened for travel July 4, 1874. It is one thousand feet long by one hundred feet wide, and is fifty-two feet above mean water-mark. It consists of five spans constructed of Pratt trusses. The roadway is of granite blocks, and is sixty-seven and a half feet wide; and the sidewalks, each sixteen and a half feet wide, are paved with slate. The balustrade and cornice are ornamented with bronze panels representing birds and foliage. Under this bridge passes a carriage-way leading to the northeast portion of the Park, now called, by way of distinction, the East Park. The cars of the Girard Avenue branch of the Fourth and Eighth Street Railway pass over this bridge, and the cars of the Union line (Fairmount branch) have their terminus in its vicinity.

Gray's Ferry Bridge, on the line of the Philadelphia, Wilmington and Baltimore Railroad, is a wooden structure (with a *draw*) across the Schuylkill at Federal Street, Gray's Ferry. The bridge is about eight hundred feet in length, and is traversed by the tracks of the Baltimore Railroad, besides having a roadway for vehicles and pedestrians. Gray's Ferry Bridge is reached by the Pine Street cars (Gray's Ferry branch); and the cars on Woodland Avenue (Darby Road) convey passengers within a few squares of the bridge; lines running north and south con-

nect with the Pine Street cars, by *exchange tickets* (price nine cents), for Gray's Ferry.

Market Street Bridge. The present bridge spanning the Schuylkill at Market Street is a temporary structure, built to replace the old bridge, which was burnt, November 20, 1875. The cars of the Market Street Passenger Railway cross the river on this bridge, and the Pennsylvania Railroad has a track on it for freight cars. The present temporary structure was erected by the Pennsylvania Railroad Company in twenty-one days, at a cost of $56,500. Besides the Market Street cars the bridge is accessible by the Arch Street cars, which run to Twenty-first and Arch Streets, the Walnut Street cars, which run to Twenty-third and Chestnut Streets, and the Pine Street cars (Fairmount branch), which pass Market Street at Twenty-third.

South Street Bridge, an elegant new structure of iron and stone, crossing the Schuylkill River at South Street, is, with its approaches, about two thousand five hundred feet in length. A central draw, of about one hundred and fifty feet in length, permits the passage of vessels. The bridge is accessible by the South Street cars, and the cars on Pine Street pass, by the Gray's Ferry route, to the immediate vicinity.

Wissahickon Bridges. Several bridges across the Wissahickon add to the beauty and interest of that romantic stream, among which may be mentioned the Railroad Bridge, on the line of the Norristown branch of the Reading Railroad, near the mouth of the Wissahickon; a wooden structure, four hundred and twenty feet long, and about seventy-five feet above the level of the stream. Three and a half miles above its mouth the stream is crossed by a beautiful structure, called the Pipe Bridge, six hundred and eighty-four feet long, and one hundred feet above the creek. The water-pipes that supply Germantown with water form the chords of the bridge, the whole being bound together with wrought-iron. It was designed by Frederick Graff, and constructed under his superintendence. A hundred yards above this is a wooden bridge, near which is the Devil's Pool, a basin in Cresheim Creek; and farther up, at Valley Green, a stone bridge crosses the Wissahickon.

CARPENTERS' HALL.

On the south side of Chestnut Street, about midway between Third and Fourth Streets, an iron railing guards the passage-way to a building which deserves more than any other the proud title of the cradle of American Independence. It is Carpenters' Hall, the place where, as an inscription on the wall proudly testifies, "Henry, Hancock, and Adams inspired the Delegates of the Colonies with Nerve and Sinew for the Toils of War;" the place where the first Continental Congress met, and where the famous "first prayer in Congress" was delivered by Parson Duché on the morning after the news of the bombardment of Boston had been received, and men knew that the war was indeed "inevitable." Here the first Provincial Assembly held its sittings, to be succeeded by the British troops, and afterwards by the first United States Bank, and still later by the Bank of Pennsylvania.

Built in 1770, Carpenters' Hall was at first intended only for the uses

CONNECTING RAILROAD BRIDGE, FAIRMOUNT PARK.

of the Society of Carpenters, by whom it was founded. Its central location, however, caused it to be used for the meetings of delegates to the Continental Congress, and for other public purposes; and when no longer needed for these, it passed from tenant to tenant, until it degenerated into an auction-room. Then the Company of Carpenters, taking patriotic counsel, resumed control of it, fitted it up to represent as nearly as might be its appearance in Revolutionary days, and it is now kept as a sacred relic. The walls are hung with interesting mementos of the times that tried men's souls. The door is always open to the patriotic visitor.

CARPENTERS' HALL.

Visitors from the northern and northwestern sections of the city reach Carpenters' Hall by the cars on Second Street, which, at Chestnut Street, pass within two squares; by the Fourth Street cars, which, at Chestnut Street, pass within a few doors; by the cars of the Union line (Market Street branch), which, at Fourth and Market Streets, pass within two squares; by the Green Street cars, which pass Fourth and Chestnut Streets, a few doors distant; and by the Race Street cars, which pass at Second and Chestnut Streets, within two squares; from the west the Market Street cars pass at Fourth Street, within two squares, the Chestnut Street cars pass the entrance, and the Spruce Street cars convey passengers to Third and Walnut Streets, two squares distant; from the south the cars on Third and Fifth Streets pass at Chestnut, within short distances of the Hall.

CEMETERIES.

Of the many beautiful cemeteries in which repose the dead of the great city, we direct the visitor to a few of the more prominent ones, and assure him that a visit to them will be a source of gratification. We use the word advisedly, for few more pleasant spots can be found in the vicinity of Philadelphia than its burial-places, fitted up as they are with equal taste and elegance.

Cathedral Cemetery, the great burying-ground of the Roman Catholic denomination, is located on Forty-eighth Street, between Girard Avenue and Wyalusing Street, in West Philadelphia. It was consecrated to the purposes of sepulture in 1849, being named after the Cathedral of St. Peter and St. Paul, which was then building. The cemetery includes forty-three acres, and contains some elegant monuments. It is reached by the cars of the Hestonville, Mantua and Fairmount Railway, which connect at Fairmount with the various other lines leading to or from the eastern section of the city; the cars of the Market Street line also pass, at Fiftieth and Haverford Streets, within a few squares of the cemetery.

Laurel Hill. Laurel Hill Cemetery is confessedly the leading cemetery of Philadelphia in size, location, and beauty of adornment. It is situated on a sloping hillside bordering on the Schuylkill; the extensive grounds are skillfully laid out; and the monuments and other decorations are as elaborate as affection could suggest or munificence bestow. The ground is divided into three sections, known as North, South, and Central Laurel Hill,—the last being the most recently added of the three. The plan of the company by which this cemetery was established was to provide for its patrons a resting-place which should be theirs forever, without fear of molestation or disturbance by the ever-lengthening city streets and the ever-growing city trade, and which they might therefore ornament freely with substantial and enduring monuments. The idea was well carried out in the selection of a site little available for business purposes, and now secured forever by its incorporation within the bounds of Fairmount Park; and it was quickly appreciated by the citizens. The result is shown in the present appearance of the grounds, and in the fact that South Laurel Hill and two other sections of ground have been added. On the opposite side of the river, about a mile above the original Laurel Hill, is West Laurel Hill Cemetery, an institution entirely distinct from the original, and controlled by a separate corporation, but yet owned and officered to a large extent by the same individuals. In its arrangement the fundamental idea of an isolated and permanent burial-place has been kept strictly in view. The cars of the Ridge Avenue Passenger Railway convey visitors to the entrance of the cemetery, and the steamers on the Schuylkill River have landings there.

Monument Cemetery. Monument Cemetery, which was founded in 1837, two years after Laurel Hill, is situated at Broad and Berks Streets, and is remarkable for a fine granite monument to the joint memories of Washington and Lafayette, which stands in the centre, and gives name to the cemetery. It is reached from the southern section of the city by the Nineteenth Street cars and by the Fifteenth Street cars, and by lines running east and west, which exchange with these. Still nearer Laurel Hill are MOUNT PEACE, MOUNT VERNON, GLENWOOD, MECHANICS', ODD FELLOWS', and several other cemeteries, all of which are reached by the Ridge Avenue cars.

Mount Moriah. Mount Moriah Cemetery is on Kingsessing Avenue, about three miles from Market Street, and is reached by the Darby line of horse cars running out Walnut Street. It is quite large, and is very liberally supplied with both natural and artificial attractions.

West Laurel Hill. West Laurel Hill Cemetery is the latest enterprise of the kind connected with the city, having been incorporated

LIEUTENANT GREBLE'S MONUMENT.

in November, 1869. It is situated on the west side of the Schuylkill, in Montgomery County, a short distance from the boundary-line of the incorporated city.

At present West Laurel Hill contains one hundred and ten acres, but the charter permits its increase to three hundred acres. Under the management of persons long familiar with the work done at the original Laurel Hill, it is rapidly assuming a beautiful appearance. It is reached by the cars of the Philadelphia and Reading Railroad from Broad and Callowhill Streets, stopping at Pencoyd Station.

Woodland Cemetery, one of the most attractive rural burying-grounds in the city, is situated on Darby Road, and is accessible by the cars of the Darby branch of the Chestnut and Walnut Street line, which pass the entrance at Thirty-ninth Street. Of the many imposing monuments in this cemetery are the beautiful mausoleum of the Drexel family, which is noted for its elegance of design—being the handsomest structure of its kind in this country—and its fine location, and the chaste monument erected to the memory of Lieutenant John T. Greble, the first officer of the regular army to fall in the Rebellion.

CENTENNIAL EXHIBITION.

THE Centennial grounds, in Fairmount Park, cover 236 acres, and extend from the foot of GEORGE'S HILL (q. v.) almost to the Schuylkill River, and north to Columbia Bridge and Belmont Mansion (see BELMONT). They can be reached directly by the following lines of horse-cars: Chestnut and Walnut, Market, Arch, Race and Vine, and Girard Avenue; and by steam-cars via the Reading Railroad and the Pennsylvania Railroad.

Approaching the Exhibition grounds by way of Elm Avenue, we first enter the MAIN BUILDING, which is 1880 feet long, 464 feet wide, 48 feet to the cornice, and 70 feet to the roof-tree, covering an area of 20 acres. At each corner a square tower runs up to a level with the roof, and four more are clustered in the centre of the edifice, and rise to the height of 120 feet from a base of 48 feet square. These flank a central dome 120 feet square at base, and springing on iron trusses of delicate and graceful design to an apex 96 feet above the pavement,—the exact elevation of the interior of the old Capitol rotunda. The transept, the intersection of which with the nave forms this pavilion, is 416 feet long. On each side of it is another of the same length and 100 feet in width, with aisles of 48 feet each. Longitudinally, the divisions of the interior correspond with these transverse lines. A nave 120 feet wide and 1832 feet long—said to be unique for combined length and width—is accompanied by two side avenues 100 feet wide, and as many aisles 48 feet wide. An exterior aisle 24 feet wide, and as many high to a half-roof or clere-story, passes round the whole building except where interrupted by the main entrances in the centres of the sides and ends, and a number of minor ones between. The iron columns supporting the roof number, in all, 672.

A breadth of 30 feet is left to the main promenades along and athwart,

SECTION OF THE MAIN EXHIBITION BUILDING.

of 15 feet to the principal ones on either side, and of 10 feet to all the others.

Four miles of water- and drainage-pipe underlie the 21½ acres of plank floor in this building. The pillars and trusses contain 3600 tons of iron. The cost of the building was $1,600,000.

Leaving the Main Building at its west end, we pass to MACHINERY HALL, little smaller than its neighbor, it being 1402 feet long by 360 feet wide, covering an area of 14 acres. The main cornice is 40 feet in height upon the outside; the interior height being 70 feet in the two main longitudinal avenues and 40 feet in the one central and two side aisles. The avenues are each 90 feet in width, and the aisles 60, with a space of 15 feet for free passage in the former and 10 in the latter. A transept 90 feet broad crosses the main building into that for hydraulics, bringing up against a tank 60 by 160 feet, whereinto the water-works precipitate, Versailles fashion, a cataract 35 feet high by 40 feet wide.

The external appearance of Machinery Hall is pleasing. The one central and four terminal towers, with their open, kiosk-like tops, are really graceful, and the slender spires which surmount them are preferable to the sheet-iron turrets. The cost of the construction of Machinery Hall was $800,000. In the centre of the immense hall stands the "Corliss engine," of 1400 horse-power, and the largest hitherto known.

Following Belmont Avenue, the Appian Way of the Centennial, to the northwest, we penetrate a mob of edifices, fountains, restaurants, government offices, etc., and reach the AGRICULTURAL BUILDING,—the palace of the farmer. The building is worthy of a Centennial agricultural fair: 540 by 820 feet, with 10¼ acres under roof, it equals the halls of a dozen State cattle-shows. The

HORTICULTURAL HALL.

style is Gothic, the three transepts looking like those of as many cathedrals. The nave is 125 feet wide, with an elevation of 75 feet. The materials are wood and glass. The contract price was $300,000. From this exhibition we cross a ravine, and ascend another eminence to HORTICULTURAL HALL.

No site could have been more happily chosen for this beautiful congress-hall of flowers. It occupies a bluff that overlooks the Schuylkill 100 feet below to the eastward, and is bounded by the deep channels of a pair of brooks equidistant on the north and south sides.

For the expression of its purpose, with all the solidity and grace consistent with that, the Moresque structure before us is not excelled by any within the grounds. Entering from the side by a neat flight of steps in dark marble, we find ourselves in a gayly-tiled vestibule 30 feet square, between forcing-houses each 100 by 30 feet. Advancing, we enter the great conservatory, 230 by 80 feet, and 55 feet high. A gallery 20 feet from the floor carries us up among the dates and cocoanuts. The decorations of this hall are in keeping with the external design. The dimensions of the building are 380 feet by 193 feet.

Outside promenades, four in number, and each 100 feet long, lead along the roofs of the forcing-houses, and contribute to the portfolio of lovely views that enriches the Park. Other prospects are offered by the upper floors of the east and west fronts; the aërial terrace embracing in all 17,000 square feet. Restaurants, reception-rooms, and offices occupy the two ends. The cost of the building was $250,000.

Leaving Horticultural Hall, we cross the bridge spanning the picturesque Landsdowne Ravine to MEMORIAL HALL, which, as its name im-

MEMORIAL HALL.

plies, contemplates indefinite durability. What Virginia and Massachusetts granite, in alliance with Pennsylvania iron, on a basis of $1,500,000, can effect in that direction, seems to have been done. The façade is in ultra-Renaissance, with arch and balustrade and open arcade. The square central tower, or what under a circular dome would be the drum, is quite in harmony with the main front in proportion and outline, and renders the unity of the building very striking. That its object, of supplying the best light for pictures and statuary, is not lost sight of, is evidenced by the fact that three-fourths of the interior space is lighted from above, and the residue has an ample supply from lofty windows. The figures of America, Art, Science, etc., stud the dome and parapet, while eagles with wings outspread decorate the four corners of the corner towers.

The eight arched windows of the corner towers, $12\frac{1}{2}$ by 34 feet, are utilized for art-display. Munich fills two with stained glass: England also claims a place in them. The iron doors of the front are inlaid with bronze panels bearing the insignia of the States.

In addition to this building, 365 by 210 feet, affording 89,000 square feet of wall-surface for pictures, an additional building of very nearly equal dimensions, or 349 by 186 feet, was found necessary to receive the contributions offered. This building is on the rear, or north side, of Memorial Hall proper, and is the first portion of the fine-art department that meets the eye of one coming from Horticultural Hall. It is built of brick, and in the interior plan closely imitates Memorial Hall.

MINOR BUILDINGS.—Directly opposite the entrance, but beyond the north line of the great halls, stands the *Judges' Pavilion*, 152 by 115 feet in extent. Next the *Women's Pavilion*, with its ground-plan blending the

WOMEN'S PAVILION.

cross and the square. Nave and transept are identical in dimensions, each being 64 by 192 feet, the four angles formed by thier intersection being nearly filled out by as many sheds 48 feet square. A cupola springs from the centre to a height of 90 feet. Near by is the *Government Build-*

GOVERNMENT BUILDING.

ing, erected to "illustrate the functions and administrative faculties of the government in time of peace, and its resources as a war-power."

PENNSYLVANIA BUILDING.

The building, business-like and capable-looking, was erected in a style and with a degree of economy creditable to the officers of the board selected from the Departments of **War**, Agriculture, the Treasury,

Navy, Interior, and Post-Office, and from the Smithsonian Institution. Appended to it are smaller structures for the illustration of hospital and

NEW JERSEY BUILDING.

laboratory work. In the rear of the lordly palace of the Federal government stand the humbler tenements of *the States*, embracing Ohio, Indiana, Illinois, Wisconsin, Michigan, New Hampshire, Connecticut, Massachusetts, Delaware, New Jersey, and Kansas. Pennsylvania's picturesque building stands on the south side of Fountain Avenue, and her Educational Department is represented by another building, near Memorial Hall.

These buildings are all of wood, with the exception of that of Ohio, which exhibits some of the fine varieties of stone furnished by the quarries of that State. All have two floors, save the Massachusetts cottage, a quaint affair modeled after the homes of the past. The State of New York plays orderly sergeant, and stands in front of Delaware. She is very fortunate in the site assigned her, at the junction of State Avenue with several promenades, and her building is not unworthy so prominent a position.

From the Empire State we step into the domain of Old England. Three of her rural homesteads rise before us, red-tiled, many-gabled,

NEW YORK BUILDING.

and lattice-windowed. It is a bit of the island peopled by some of the islanders. *Great Britain's* headquarters are made particularly attractive,

BRITISH BUILDINGS.

not more by the picturesqueness of the buildings than by the extent and completeness of her exhibit.

Japan is a close neighbor to England. Besides the dwelling for its employés, the Japanese government has erected in a more central situa-

OHIO BUILDING.

tion, close to the Judges' Pavilion, another building. The style of this

JAPANESE BUILDING.

is equally characteristic. Together, the two structures do what houses may toward making us acquainted with the public and private ménage of Japan.

FOUNTAIN OF THE CATHOLIC TOTAL ABSTINENCE UNION.

The delicacy of the Asiatic touch is exemplified in the wood-carving upon the doorways and pediments of the Japanese dwelling. Ara-

SWEDISH SCHOOL-HOUSE.

besques and reproductions of subjects from Nature are executed with a clearness and precision such as we are accustomed to admire on the lacquered-ware cabinets and the bronzes of Japan.

SPANISH BUILDING.

The neat little *Swedish School-house*, of unpainted wood, that stands next to the main Japanese building, is attractive for its peculiarity of construction. It was erected by Swedish carpenters.

The contemporaries and ancient foes of the Northmen have a memorial in the beautiful Alhambra-like edifice of the Spanish government. *Spain* has no architecture so distinctive as that of the Moors, and the selection of their style for the present purpose was in good taste. Seated not far from the Spanish buildings, and side by side with that of *Brazil*, are the handsome *German* buildings. The larger building is appropriated especially to the use of the German Commissioners; the two smaller ones are devoted chiefly to the exhibition of wines and chemicals.

France is represented by three small structures,—one for the general use of the French Commission, another for the special display of bronzes, and the third for another art-manufacture for which France is becoming eminent,—stained glass. This overflowing from her great and closely-occupied area in Memorial Hall, hard by, indicates the wealth of France in art. She is largely represented, moreover, in another outlying province of the same domain,—photography.

Photographic Hall, an offshoot from Memorial Hall. and lying between it and the Main Building, is quite a solid structure, 258 feet by 107, with 19,000 feet of wall space.

CHURCHES.

It is not remarkable in this age that the most ambitious effort of monumental art upon the Exposition grounds should have taken the shape

GERMAN BUILDING.

of a fountain. The erection is due to the energy and public spirit of the *Catholic Total Abstinence Union*. The site chosen is at the extreme western end of Machinery Hall. It looks along Fountain Avenue to the Horticultural Building. Mated thus with that fine building, it becomes a permanent feature of the Park. Other fountains are scattered through the grounds, but they are of comparatively modest proportions.

Another contribution in the cause of art is the statue, in bronze, of Dr. Witherspoon, the only clerical Signer, which stands on the east side of the grounds.

We have now briefly described the most important buildings which stand out prominently in the midst of a host of structures of infinite variety of size, shape, and purpose, among which restaurants of various nationalities are especially noticeable. But in a work necessarily so condensed as this it is impossible to enumerate all of these structures, and, indeed, we doubt if any description would convey an adequate impression of the scene : suffice it to say that they notably exceed the corresponding array at any of the European Expositions.

CHURCHES.

Philadelphia has within her limits nearly six hundred religious organizations, of which over five hundred possess church buildings of their own. The following may be regarded as the representative churches of their respective denominations:

BAPTIST.

Berean. A handsome brown-stone building, on Chestnut Street, near Fortieth. The Walnut Street cars pass the door.

BETH-EDEN CHURCH.

Beth-Eden, at Broad and Spruce Streets. One of the finest church edifices in the city; built of serpentine stone with variegated stone trimmings and stained glass windows.

Fifth Baptist. A Gothic brown-stone church, at the northwest corner of Eighteenth and Spring Garden Streets. The cars on the Fairmount branch of the Union line pass the church.

First Baptist, at the northwest corner of Broad and Arch Streets. A handsome structure, built of brown stone, with a steeple two hundred and twenty-five feet in height.

Fourth Baptist, corner of Fifth and Buttonwood Streets; having a semi-circular front and a tower one hundred and eighty-eight feet high.

Memorial Baptist, corner of Broad and Master Streets. An elegant new structure of unique design, built in the form of an amphitheatre; seating capacity, fourteen hundred.

Tabernacle Baptist, on Chestnut Street, above Eighteenth. An imposing structure with a semi-circular front, supported by stone pillars; it has a steeple two hundred and thirteen feet in height.

CONGREGATIONAL.

Central Congregational Church, corner of Eighteenth and Green Streets, is a new and handsome stone edifice. The interior is spacious,

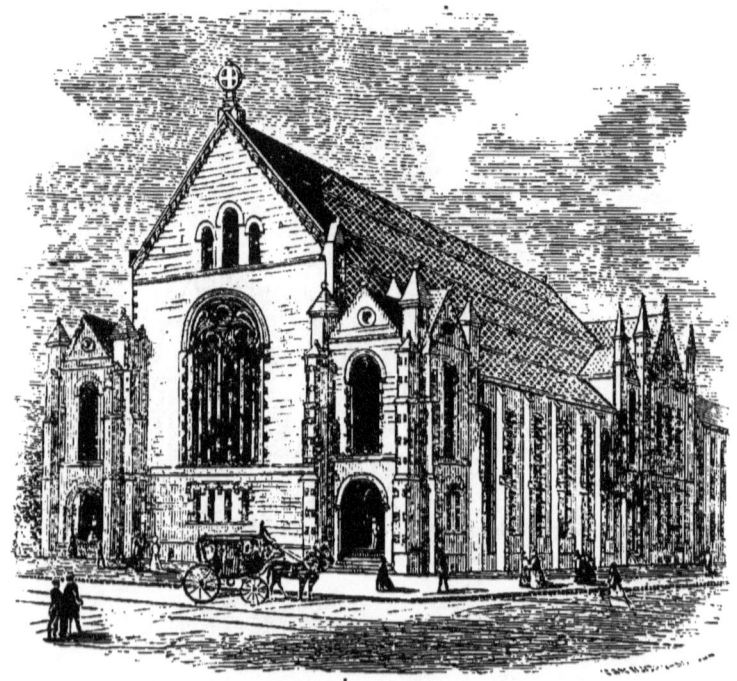

CENTRAL CONGREGATIONAL CHURCH.

and affords ample accommodations for a large congregation. The Central was the first Congregational Church successfully established in Philadelphia.

CHURCHES.

FRIENDS.

The Society of Friends (often called Quakers) is now divided into two branches, known as the "Orthodox" and "Hicksite" branches. They have fourteen "meeting-houses" in the city, mostly plain substantial brick buildings surrounded by high brick walls. The principal houses of the "Orthodox" branch are at Sixth and Noble Streets, Fourth and Arch Streets, and Twelfth Street below Market; those of the "Hicksite" branch at Race above Fifteenth Street, Girard Avenue and Seventeenth Street, Fourth and Green Streets, and Ninth and Spruce Streets.

HEBREW.

Mikve Israel. This congregation occupies a commodious brick structure on Seventh Street, between Arch and Race Streets, and is said to be the oldest Hebrew Church organization in the city. It was founded as early as the middle of the last century.

Rodef Sholem, the most celebrated of the Jewish Synagogues in the city, is situated at the southeast corner of Broad and Mount Vernon Streets. The building is a fine specimen of Saracenic architecture of stone of various colors, with elegant interior finish, and a steeple one hundred and twenty feet in height.

LUTHERAN.

Holy Communion (ENGLISH LUTHERAN), on the southwest corner of Broad and Arch Streets, is an elegant structure of green stone varied with stone trimmings of other colors. The style is semi-castellated, after the German. When completed, the church will be one of the finest in the city, and the entire cost will be over $200,000.

Saint John's (ENGLISH LUTHERAN), on the north side of Race Street, below Sixth, is a fine brick structure built early in the present century, and considered when erected one of the handsomest churches in Philadelphia. Rev. Philip F. Mayer, D.D., was for more than fifty years pastor of this congregation.

Saint Mark's (ENGLISH LUTHERAN) is situated on Spring Garden Street, above Thirteenth. The building is a remarkably fine structure, with a brown-stone front, and a steeple two hundred and twenty-five feet in height.

Zion (GERMAN LUTHERAN), on Franklin Street, above Race Street, (west side of Franklin Square), is a handsome brown-stone building recently erected. From the north the cars of the Union line pass the door of the church; and from the south the Eighth Street cars pass (at Race Street) within a square.

METHODIST EPISCOPAL.

The churches of this denomination number nearly one hundred, of which the following are among the principal:

Arch Street, on the southeast corner of Broad and Arch Streets. An elegant white marble structure built in the Gothic style of architecture, with a steeple two hundred and thirty-three feet in height. It is among the handsomest and most costly church edifices in the city.

Grace Church, at the northwest corner of Broad and Master Streets. The congregation at present occupies an elegant white marble chapel, to which it is designed to add eventually a main edifice of corresponding beauty.

Spring Garden Street Church, situated at the corner of Twentieth and Spring Garden Streets, is a large plain brown-stone building, in the early English-Gothic style. The cars of the Fairmount branch of the Union line pass the church.

Saint George's, on Fourth Street, between Race and Vine, is a plain rough-cast brick building, noted as being the oldest Methodist Church in the city.

Trinity Methodist, on Eighth Street, above Race, was for many years one of the leading churches of the denomination.

MORAVIAN.

First Church, situated at the corner of Franklin and Wood Streets, is the principal church of this denomination. It is a neat edifice, built in the Gothic style, of brick, rough cast, and was consecrated in 1856. The cars of the Union line from the north pass the church.

NEW CHURCH (Swedenborgian).

THE **First New Jerusalem Society,** the principal of the three New Church organizations in the city, has its temple at Broad and Brandywine Streets, above Spring Garden Street. The cars on the Fairmount branch of the Union line convey passengers to Broad and Spring Garden Streets, near the temple. The building is a tasty structure, neatly furnished within.

PRESBYTERIAN.

Of the one hundred or more Presbyterian Churches in the city, the following are among the most important:

Alexander, on the northeast corner of Nineteenth and Green Streets, is a fine stone structure in the Gothic style of architecture, with a spire two hundred feet in height.

Bethany, at Twenty-second and Bainbridge Streets, is a plain substantial structure of Trenton brown stone, with a front on Bainbridge Street of one hundred and twelve feet, and a depth of one hundred and eighty-five feet to Pemberton Street. It has a seating capacity of two thousand. Adjoining is the remarkable Sunday-school building belonging to the Church, fronting on Twenty-second, Bainbridge, and Pemberton Streets, and having a breadth of one hundred and thirty-eight feet by a depth of one hundred and eighty-five feet. It possesses accommodations for nearly three thousand persons, and is said to be the largest building in the United States devoted to Sunday-school purposes. The Pine Street cars convey passengers to the immediate vicinity of the church.

Calvary, a handsome brown-stone building on Locust Street, above Fifteenth, is built in the Gothic style of architecture, with two steeples each one hundred and thirty-five feet in height.

Chambers' Presbyterian, at the corner of Broad and Sansom Streets, below Chestnut. The building is a spacious structure, with a fine Corinthian portico.

Fifth, commonly called **Arch Street**. A plain brick structure on Arch Street, above Tenth; one of the most commodious church buildings in the city. The Arch Street cars pass the door, and the Tenth and Eleventh Streets and Ridge Avenue cars convey passengers to within a short distance of the church.

First Presbyterian, corner of Locust and Seventh Streets. A brick edifice, rough cast, with an Ionic portico, and a cupola over one hundred feet high. This was the first Presbyterian Church organized in this State, having been formed in 1698, under the ministration of Rev. Jedediah Andrews, of New England, who remained its pastor for more than half a century. Other eminent divines were his successors, among whom the best known to the present generation was the late Rev. Albert Barnes, who preached here for thirty-eight years.

North Broad Street, at the corner of Broad and Green Streets, is a handsome brown-stone building seventy feet front by one hundred and fifteen feet deep, with a steeple two hundred and twenty-two feet in height.

Second Presbyterian, at the southeast corner of Twenty-first and Walnut Streets, is a handsome variegated stone structure, the interior walls being finished with English brick. Elaborate carvings adorn the building within and without, and the tower is to be surmounted by a spire two hundred feet high. The congregation was first formed in 1743, under the ministration of George Whitefield, and had their first church building at Third and Arch Streets. Subsequently they occupied a church on Seventh Street, below Arch. The present building was dedicated in 1872. The Walnut Street cars pass the church.

Tabernacle Presbyterian, on Broad Street, above Chestnut, is built in the Grecian style of architecture, and has a portico with eight columns.

West Arch Street Church, on the corner of Eighteenth and Arch Streets, is a remarkably fine specimen of church architecture of the Corinthian order, with ornamented cupolas at the front corners one hundred and fifteen feet high, and a central dome one hundred and seventy feet high.

PROTESTANT EPISCOPAL.

There are in the city about one hundred churches of this denomination, many of them of much celebrity. The principal among them are the following:

Christ Church, a unique brick structure on Second Street, above Market, erected and enlarged at various times during the early part of the last century, celebrated for having been the place of worship for

CHURCHES.

many distinguished men, prior to and during the Revolution. Latterly the interior has been modernized somewhat, but the structure retains much of its original quaintness. The steeple contains a chime of eight bells. The burying-ground of this church is at the southeast corner of Fifth and Arch Streets, where lie the remains of Dr. Franklin, and many other distinguished men of the olden time.

Epiphany, at Fifteenth and Chestnut Streets. A brick edifice, rough cast, with a Doric portico in front. The church has a spacious interior, and accommodates a large congregation.

Gloria Dei (OLD SWEDES'), the oldest church in the city, is situated on Swanson Street, below Christian. It is a brick structure, and was dedicated in the year 1700. The congregation was originally Swedish Lutheran, but now belongs to the Protestant Episcopal communion. The Second Street cars pass near the church.

Holy Trinity, at Walnut and Nineteenth Streets. An elegant brown-stone structure, in the Gothic style, with a tower one hundred and fifty feet in height.

Saint Andrews, Eighth Street, above Spruce. A brick structure, rough cast, with a Corinthian portico and front presenting an imposing appearance.

Saint Clement's, at Twentieth and Cherry Streets, is a handsome brown-stone structure in the French-Gothic style. The Arch Street cars pass at Twentieth near the church, and the Nineteenth Street cars pass at Cherry Street, one square distant.

Saint James's. An elegant stone structure, in the Gothic style, at Twenty-second and Walnut Streets. The Walnut Street cars pass the church.

Saint Mark's, on Locust Street, above Sixteenth. A fine brown-stone structure in the Gothic style, with a beautiful tower and spire one hundred and seventy feet in height. This church is considered the finest specimen of Gothic church architecture in the city.

Saint Paul's, on Third Street, below Walnut, was built in 1761, and is chiefly noticeable on account of its antiquity.

Saint Peter's, at Third and Pine Streets, is among the most interesting of the old-time church edifices. It was erected about the middle of the last century, and still retains many of its original architectural features. It has a spire two hundred and eighteen feet in height, in which is a chime of eight bells. General Washington was once an attendant at St. Peter's. In the burial-ground connected with the church are the graves of many men distinguished in their time.

Saint Stephen's, on Tenth Street, between Chestnut and Market Streets, is an imposing brick rough-cast structure with octagonal towers, in which is a chime of bells. A beautiful white marble monument erected by Edward Shippen Burd to the memory of members of his family, occupying a small apartment opening from the body of the church, and a monument to Mr. Burd placed in the interior near the entrance, attract much attention as works of art.

REFORMED.

Of the Reformed denominations there are about twenty churches, the principal of which are—

Christ Church (REFORMED GERMAN), on Green Street, between Fifteenth and Sixteenth Streets. A comely structure, with a tall and graceful spire.

First Reformed (GERMAN), on Race Street, between Third and Fourth Streets. Founded in 1732.

First Reformed (DUTCH), at the corner of Seventh and Spring Garden Streets. An imposing structure with a handsome portico on the front. The cars of the Union line pass this church.

Second Reformed (DUTCH), situated on Seventh Street, above Brown. A brick structure, with a Grecian portico and a neatly furnished interior.

ROMAN CATHOLIC.

Of this denomination there are about fifty churches in the city, the congregations being for the most part very large. The principal church edifices are—

Cathedral of Saint Peter and Saint Paul, on Eighteenth Street, above Race, opposite Logan Square. The corner-stone of this magnificent building, the finest Catholic church in the city, and up to the present date the finest in the United States, was laid by the Right Rev. F. P. Kenrick, September 6, 1846, and it was opened for divine service November, 1864. The edifice is one hundred and thirty-six feet front, two hundred and sixteen feet deep, and two hundred and ten feet in total height. The interior of the building is cruciform, and is designed in the most elaborate Roman-Corinthian style. The floor is of marble, supported by arches of brick. Elaborate paintings decorate the walls and ceilings. Four columns, sixty feet high and six feet in diameter, constitute an imposing front of the Roman-Corinthian order, surmounted by a frieze bearing the inscription, "*Ad majorum Dei gloriam.*"

Church of the Assumption, north side of Spring Garden Street, near Twelfth, is a brown-stone Gothic structure with two spires, each one hundred and sixty feet in height.

Saint Augustine's. A plain brick structure, on the west side of Fourth Street, below Vine, having a steeple one hundred and eighty-eight feet in height. The original church building was destroyed by fire during the Native American riots in 1844.

Saint John the Evangelist's, on Thirteenth Street, above Chestnut. A rough-cast brick building in the Gothic style, with towers in front. The structure is large, and the interior is decorated with fine paintings.

Saint Mary's, on Fourth Street, above Spruce. A plain spacious brick structure, erected in 1763, being the second Roman Catholic church erected in the city. It was for many years the Cathedral church.

Saint Joseph's, on Willing's Alley, between Third and Fourth

CATHEDRAL OF ST. PETER AND ST. PAUL.

D

Streets, south of Walnut Street. A plain brick structure, on the site of the first Roman Catholic church erected in Pennsylvania. The original church was erected about the year 1732.

Saint Peter's, at Fifth Street and Girard Avenue. A large brick rough-cast structure of the Roman-Corinthian style, with a spire two hundred and thirty-five feet in height. The main apartment of the church will accommodate two thousand people, besides which there are a chapel and Sunday-school rooms, and adjoining parish schools and monastic buildings. The church belongs to the order of Redemptionists.

UNITARIAN.

First Unitarian, at Tenth and Locust Streets, below Walnut. A brick rough-cast structure, with a handsome marble front and a portico in the Grecian-Doric style. The celebrated Dr. Priestley was the founder of this society, near the beginning of the present century, and for more than fifty years the Rev. William H. Furness, D.D., was pastor.

UNIVERSALIST.

Church of the Messiah, on Locust Street, between Thirteenth and Broad Streets. A rough-cast brick building, in the Gothic style.

Church of the Restoration. A brown-stone structure recently erected on Master Street, between Sixteenth and Seventeenth Streets.

First Universalist. A plain brick structure, on Lombard Street, above Fourth Street.

CITY HALL.

The new City Hall, popularly known as "The Public Buildings," now in course of erection at the junction of Broad and Market Streets, is by far the most notable building in Philadelphia, and among the most notable in the United States. It was begun on the 10th of August, 1871, and, it is estimated, will cost ten years' time and ten million dollars to complete. When finished, it will be the largest building in America, and probably the highest in the world, being four hundred and eighty-six and a half feet in length, north and south, and four hundred and seventy feet in width, east and west. The central tower will rise to the height of four hundred and fifty feet, a greater height than any other spire in the world, the crowning feature being a statue of William Penn twenty feet in height. The area actually covered is nearly four and a half acres, not including a court-yard in the centre, two hundred feet square. Around the whole will be a grand avenue two hundred and five feet wide on the northern front, and one hundred and thirty-five feet on the others. The general style of the building is the Renaissance, modified to suit the purposes for which it is required. The basement story is of fine white granite, and the superstructure of white marble from the Lee quarries, the whole strongly backed with brick and made perfectly fireproof. The structure will contain five hundred and twenty rooms, and afford ample provision for the present and future needs of its occupants. Its erection is in charge

NEW CITY HALL ("PUBLIC BUILDINGS").

of a Commission, and the architect who drew the plan and has charge of the work is John McArthur, Jr.

The cars on Market, Arch, Chestnut, and Walnut Streets pass at Broad Street, near the immediate locality of this building, and from the northern and southern sections of the city lines of cars connecting with these lines by *exchange tickets* (price nine cents) convey passengers to the vicinity.

CUSTOM-HOUSE.

The United States Custom-House, on the south side of Chestnut Street, between Fourth and Fifth, has two fronts, one on Chestnut, the other on Library Street, each ornamented with eight fluted Doric columns, twenty-seven feet high and four feet six inches in diameter, supporting a heavy entablature. It is in imitation of the Parthenon at Athens, and is one of the purest specimens of Doric architecture in the country. The building was completed in 1824, having cost $500,000, and was formerly the United States Bank. It is now used by the United States Sub-Treasury and Custom-House officers.

This locality is reached from the northern section of the city by the cars on Fourth Street, which, at Chestnut Street, pass within a few doors of the building; by the cars on Sixth Street, which, at Chestnut Street, pass within two squares; by the cars of the Union line (Market Street branch), which, at Fourth and Market Streets, pass one square distant, and by the Green Street cars, which pass at Fourth and Chestnut Streets, a few doors distant; from the west the Market Street cars pass at Fourth and Market Streets, one square distant; the Chestnut Street cars pass the door, and the Spruce Street cars, at Fourth and Spruce Streets, pass within two squares; from the south the Third Street cars pass at Third and Chestnut Streets, within two squares, and the Fifth Street cars, at Chestnut, pass near the building.

Just above the Custom-House is the old Post-Office, a handsome marble building. Although the facilities of this department were greatly increased when this office was built, not long since, the rapid growth of its business now calls for greater space, and, to supply the want, a new building is being erected at the corner of Ninth and Chestnut Streets, for which an appropriation of $3,000,000 has been made.

Deaf and Dumb Asylum. See HOSPITALS AND ASYLUMS.

DELAWARE RIVER.

Prominent among the attractions of Philadelphia is the Delaware River front, with its miles of wharves and storehouses, its numerous ocean steamers and sailing vessels, and its busy ferry-boats and other river craft plying hither and thither. Excursions on the Delaware by steamer, up the river to Burlington and Trenton and intermediate places, and down the river to Wilmington and other points on the Delaware Bay, are favorite methods of recreation. As might be supposed, this river, with its broad stream, deep channel, and abrupt bank, is the chosen home of the shipping interest, while the Schuylkill is still waiting for the time to come when its shores will be needed to relieve the

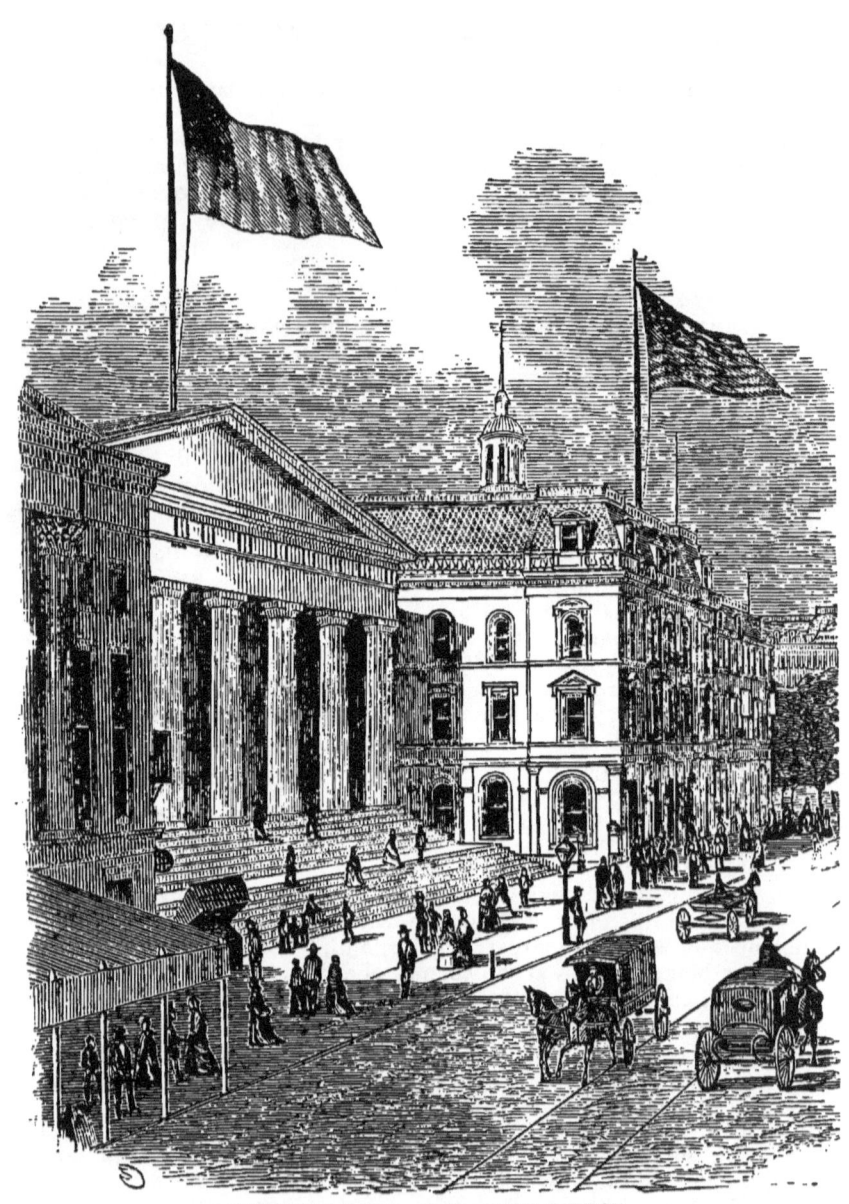

CUSTOM-HOUSE AND POST-OFFICE.

eastern wharves. Important points on the river are reached from the western section of the city by the Callowhill Street cars, which convey passengers to Front and Vine Streets (the ferry of the Camden and Atlantic Railroad); by the Race Street cars, which pass along Second

VIEW ON THE DELAWARE.

Street to Walnut; by the Ridge Avenue cars, which approach the River at Second and Arch Streets; by the Arch Street cars, which also run to Second and Arch Streets; by the cars of the Union line, which by the Market Street branch run to Front and Market Streets, and by the Navy Yard branch run to Front and Wharton Streets; by the Market Street cars, which also run to Front and Market Streets; by the Chestnut Street cars, which run to Second and Chestnut Streets; by the Spruce Street cars, which convey passengers to Third and Walnut Streets; and by the Lombard Street cars, which run to Front and Lombard Streets.

Dental Colleges. See MEDICAL SCHOOLS.

Depots. See RAILROAD DEPOTS.

FAIRMOUNT.

FAIRMOUNT PARK.

FAIRMOUNT PARK, new though it is, has already attained a reputation second only to that of Central Park, New York, and only second to that because Fairmount is not yet old enough to be as widely known.

Fairmount Park needs no eulogist. It speaks for itself; and the stranger who, with this book for his guide, will spend a summer day— or, better still, a week—in leisurely and appreciative exploration of its hills and dales, its leafy woodlands and sunny slopes, its rippling streams and placid river, its dewy sunrise and dreamy sunset, and the glory of its moonlight vistas, will permit no tongue to sound its praises louder than his own.

The Park now contains nearly three thousand acres, being more than three times as large as the New York Central Park. It is dedicated to be a public pleasure-ground forever, and, under the management of a Board of Commissioners, is rapidly growing in beauty and interest.

The visitor will take a street-car on Pine, Arch, or Vine Street,—all of which lines run to the bridge at the lower end of the Park, while the two last named connect and run on to George's Hill, at its western extremity; or a car of the Green and Coates Streets line, which runs from Fourth Street, *via* Walnut, Eighth, and Fairmount Avenue, to the

Fairmount Avenue entrance; or a yellow car of the Union line, passing up Ninth Street and landing him at the Brown Street entrance; or a Ridge Avenue car, which will carry him to the East Park; or, if well up town, a Poplar Street or Girard Avenue car, which will deposit him at Brown Street and Girard Avenue respectively. The Lancaster Avenue branch of the Chestnut and Walnut Streets line runs to the Centennial grounds in the West Park, and a branch of the Market Street line extends to the same point. All these termini, except the extreme western and northern ones, are in the immediate vicinity of Fairmount Water-Works, at the lower end of the Park. Another route is by the Park accommodation trains of the Philadelphia and Reading Railroad, which in summer run every hour during the day, and carry passengers from the depot at Thirteenth and Callowhill Streets to Belmont, on the west side of the Schuylkill. Accommodation trains on the Pennsylvania Railroad also run to Hestonville, within a short walk of George's Hill, at the western end of the Park.

Lastly, the visitor can hire a carriage by the day, and make the tour of the Park without fatigue or difficulty; and for mere sight-seeing this is much the best way.

Entering the Park at the lower entrance, we step at once into the grounds pertaining to the Schuylkill Water-Works; and the works themselves are contained in the building, or rather group of buildings, just before us. These works were first put in operation in 1822, though the city was first supplied with water from the Schuylkill in 1799. Enormous engines worked by water-power force water from a dam in the river to the top of a hill in front of the building,—the original "Faire-Mount,"—where it is held in a distributing reservoir. The same works supply a reservoir on Corinthian Avenue, near Girard College. From a piazza in the rear, a good view is obtained of the new and elegant "double deck" iron truss bridge which has taken the place of the once celebrated Wire Bridge. (See BRIDGES.)

The grounds immediately surrounding the buildings of the Water-Works contain several fountains and pieces of statuary. The monument in our cut is that of Frederick Graff, the designer and first engineer of the works. Just above the Water-Works is a little dock, whence in summer miniature steamers ply incessantly on the river, stopping at all points of interest on their route.

The main drive of the Park begins at Green Street, passing, just inside of the entrance, a building designed for an art gallery, and thence running down nearly to the bank of the Schuylkill.

Next, crossing an open space ornamented by a bronze statue of Lincoln, erected by the Lincoln Monument Association, in the fall of 1871, we come to another hill, covered with trees, among which go winding paths, and under which green grass and flowering shrubs combine their attractions, while around the base of the hill flowers bloom and fountains play, and the curving drive leads a glittering host of carriages. This is Lemon Hill, and on its summit is the mansion in which Robert Morris had his home during the Revolutionary struggle. Here the great financier loved to dwell. He entertained many men whose names were made illustrious by those stirring times. Hancock, Franklin, the elder Adams, members of the Continental Congress, officers of the army and navy, and many of the foremost citizens met frequently under

MONUMENT ERECTED TO THE MEMORY OF FREDERICK GRAFF.

this hospitable roof. Here, busy in peace as in war, he afterwards planned those magnificent enterprises which were his financial ruin; and from here he was led away to prison, the victim of laws equally barbarous and absurd, which, because a man could not pay what he owed, locked him up lest he might earn the means to discharge his debt.

The fortunes of the once magnificent mansion have fallen, like those of its magnificent owner. It is now a restaurant, where indifferent refreshments are dealt out at correspondingly high prices; for it is an axiom that men pay most for the worst fare.

Next, following the carriage-drive, which, beginning at the Green Street entrance, runs up the river, we come to a third hill, formerly called "Sedgely Park." Here stands a small frame building known as "Grant's Cottage," because it was used by that general as his headquarters at City Point. It was brought here at the close of the war.

From this hill there is an excellent view of the Schuylkill Water-Works, which stand in a ravine just beyond it. At its foot is the Girard Avenue Bridge, an elegant iron structure, which connects the East and West Parks. (See BRIDGES.) Under this bridge passes a carriage-way leading to the northeast portion of the Park, now called, by way of distinction, the East Park. The Connecting Railroad Bridge, as it is popularly termed (see BRIDGES), which unites the Pennsylvania Railroad

THE LINCOLN MONUMENT.

with the Camden and Amboy, raises its graceful arches a little above the Girard Avenue Bridge, and through the rocky bluff which forms its eastern abutment a short tunnel has been cut, as the only means of opening a carriage-road to the East Park. This route was opened in the summer of 1871, and developed some of the loveliest scenery in all the Park. A number of fine old country-seats were absorbed in this portion of the grounds, and they remain very nearly as their former owners left them. Here a distributing reservoir, to cover one hundred and five acres, is now being constructed. Continuing up this side of the river, we come finally to Laurel Hill Cemetery (see CEMETERIES), and then to the massive stone bridge over which the coal-trains of the Reading Railroad pass on their way to Richmond. (See BRIDGES.)

We shall, however, find more marks of improvement by crossing the Girard Avenue Bridge into the West Park.

Below the Bridge, on the west side, is a tract called "Solitude," and in it stands an ancient house built by John Penn, son of Thomas Penn and grandson of William, and owned by his descendants until its purchase by the Park Commissioners. Just beyond this, the tall stand-pipe of the West Philadelphia Water-Works forms a conspicuous feature.

This tract, containing thirty-three acres, has been leased by the Park Commissioners to the Zoological Society of Philadelphia, which has fitted it up in a manner best suited for the maintenance and exhibition of birds and animals. (See ZOOLOGICAL GARDEN.)

ENTRANCE AT EGGLESFIELD.

A short distance above the bridge is the Children's Play-ground, near Sweet Brier Mansion, and passing this the road enters Lansdowne and crosses the river road by a rustic bridge, from which a beautiful view of the Schuylkill is had.

Venerable pines mark the site of Lansdowne Concourse. This fine estate of Lansdowne contained two hundred acres, and was established by John Penn, "the American," whose nephew, also named John, the son of Richard Penn, built a stately mansion here, and lived in it during the Revolutionary war,—a struggle in which his sympathies were by no

SCHUYLKILL BLUFFS, BELOW EDGELY.

means with the party that was finally successful in wresting from him the noble State which was his paternal inheritance and of which he had been Governor.

Leaving the Concourse, the road skirts the base of Belmont Reservoir, and, winding round a rather steep ascent, comes out on the summit of GEORGE'S HILL (q. v.), two hundred and ten feet above high tide.

In the broad meadow which lies at the visitor's feet as he stands on George's Hill, looking eastward, is the site of the grand Centennial Exhibition (q. v.). The carriage-road next brings us to Belmont Mansion. (See BELMONT.)

Leaving Belmont, the road passes through a comparatively uninteresting section to Chamouni, with its lake and its concourse, and the northern limits of the Park. Near the lake it intersects the Falls road, and this takes us down to the Schuylkill, which we cross by a bridge, and continue up the east bank of the river to its junction with the Wissahickon, a beautiful stream now included within the limits of the Park. (See WISSAHICKON.)

FRANKLIN INSTITUTE.

FRANKLIN INSTITUTE, organized in 1824, has for its object the cultivation of applied science and the promotion of the mechanic arts. The building is a plain marble edifice, on Seventh Street, between Market and Chestnut Streets, containing a valuable scientific library, museum, and lecture-room. Lectures are delivered here on topics appropriate to the aims of the association, and occasional exhibitions of works of the mechanic arts are held under the auspices of the Institute. A periodical is published, called the *Journal of the Franklin Institute.*

GEORGE'S HILL.

An eminence near the southwest extremity of Fairmount Park, crowning an estate of eighty-three acres, the gift of Jesse and Rebecca George to the city of Philadelphia for purposes of incorporation into the Park. The summit of the Hill is two hundred and ten feet above high tide, and it possesses rare advantages of scenery and location. It is the grand objective point of pleasure-parties. Few carriages make the tour of the Park without taking George's Hill in their way, and stopping for a few moments on its summit to rest their horses and let the inmates feast their eyes on the view which lies before them,—a view bounded only by League Island and the Delaware.

This tract had been held by the George family for many generations, and, as a memorial of the generosity of the donors, this spot was named George's Hill.

GIRARD COLLEGE.

For the establishment of Girard College, a work magnificent alike in purpose, plan, and execution, Philadelphia is indebted, as for so many other benefits, to Stephen Girard.

This eccentric but benevolent man made provision in his will for the erection of a college which should accommodate not less than three hundred children, who must be poor, white, male orphans, between the ages of six and ten years. For the site of the college, Mr. Girard bequeathed an estate of forty-five acres, called Peel Hall, situated on the Ridge Road, about a mile from its junction with Ninth and Vine Streets; and here the buildings were erected, the sum of two million dollars having been provided by the founder for the establishment and support of the institution. The capacity of the present buildings is five

GIRARD COLLEGE.

hundred and fifty, and that is about the number of the inmates now.

The College proper is justly celebrated as one of the most beautiful structures of modern times, as well as the purest specimen of Grecian architecture in America.

Situated in the northwestern section of the city, it is reached by the Girard Avenue cars, which pass the grounds; by the Ridge Avenue cars, which also pass the inclosure; by the cars of the Nineteenth Street line and of the Union line, both of which convey passengers near the entrance to the College; and by the various lines crossing and exchanging with these.

HOSPITALS AND ASYLUMS.

Among the most prominent of this class of charitable institutions in Philadelphia are the following:

Blind Asylum. "Pennsylvania Institution for the Blind," located at Twentieth and Race Streets, has for its objects the instruction of the blind in the common branches of education, including music, and in such industrial pursuits as come within their capacity. The pupils often become proficient musicians, and entertaining concerts are given at the Asylum on Wednesday afternoon of each week, to which visitors are admitted on payment of a small sum. The Asylum is reached from the eastern section of the city by the Arch Street cars and by the cars on Vine Street, and from other sections by lines which connect with these routes by *exchange tickets* (price nine cents); from the south the Nineteenth Street cars pass at Race Street, one square distant, and from Fairmount the Race Street cars pass the Asylum.

Burd Orphan Asylum of St. Stephen's Church, situated three and a half miles west of Market Street bridge, is reached by the Haddington branch of the Market Street cars. The institution was founded by Mrs. Eliza Howard Burd, widow of Edward Shippen Burd, for the support of white female orphans who shall have been baptized in the Protestant Episcopal Church of Philadelphia or Pennsylvania. The buildings are of gray stone, with a front of two hundred and sixty feet, inclosed in grounds forty-five acres in extent.

Christ Church Hospital, founded by Dr. John Kearsley "for the support of poor or distressed women of the Church of England," is situated northwest of Fairmount Park; a short distance north of George's Hill, and near the junction of Belmont Road and York Street. The building is of stone, one hundred and seventy-five feet front by fifty-five feet deep, and accommodates about one hundred inmates. No public conveyance runs direct to Christ Church Hospital, but the Park accommodation trains of the Reading Railroad convey passengers from Broad and Callowhill Streets to Belmont Station, west of the Schuylkill River; from which by a walk across the Park of about half a mile the Hospital is reached.

Deaf and Dumb Asylum. "Pennsylvania Asylum for the Deaf and Dumb," on Broad Street, above Pine, is a granite building with a front on Broad Street of about one hundred feet, and neat buildings of brick recently erected, extending to Fifteenth Street. The Asylum was founded about 1820, its object being the education of deaf mutes; and so wonderful has been the success attending the efforts of the instructors that pupils entirely deaf have been taught to speak clearly words which they could not hear. Visitors are admitted to the Asylum on week-days. From the northern section of the city the cars on Thirteenth Street pass at Pine Street, one square distant; from the west the Spruce Street cars, both the Fairmount and Gray's Ferry sections, convey passengers to Broad and Spruce Streets, within one square of the Asylum; and from West Philadelphia the Chestnut Street cars and the Market Street cars pass at Broad Street, about two squares distant; from the south the Fifteenth Street cars pass the building at Pine Street; and from the east the Pine Street cars convey passengers to the building, and the Walnut Street cars pass at Broad Street, within two squares.

Episcopal Hospital. "Hospital of the Protestant Episcopal Church," in the northeast section of the city, occupies a square of ground at Front and Huntingdon Streets. It is composed of a central building and three wings, having a front of two hundred and fifty-eight feet; the depth of the main building being two hundred and fifty-six feet, and that of the wings two hundred feet. Although under the management of the Episcopal Church, the Hospital is open to patients of all creeds. Visitors reach the Hospital by the Fifth Street cars, taking the Lehigh Avenue and Powell Street branch. Railway lines running

HOSPITAL OF THE UNIVERSITY OF PENNSYLVANIA.

east and west connect with the Fifth Street cars by *exchange tickets* (price nine cents), thus rendering the Hospital accessible from all sections of the city.

Friends' Asylum for the Insane, at Frankford, one of the oldest insane retreats in the United States, is under the management of the Society of Friends. The buildings are three-storied, and have a front of three hundred feet. About seventy-five patients can be accommodated here. Visitors to the Asylum take the Fifth Street cars, and exchange at Kensington with the steam branch for Frankford.

German Hospital, situated at Girard and Corinthian Avenues, near Girard College, is a brick building about one hundred and twenty feet in length by one hundred feet in width. Accessible by the Girard Avenue branch of the Fourth and Eighth Street cars, and by other lines running north and south, which connect by *exchange tickets* (price nine cents) with the cars on Girard Avenue. The Nineteenth Street cars also pass, at Girard Avenue, within a short distance of the Hospital.

Hospital of the University of Pennsylvania, adjoining the University, occupies a plot of ground extending from Spruce to Pine Streets, and from Thirty-fourth to Thirty-sixth Streets. As originally designed the institution will consist of a central building and two wings, with an entire front of two hundred and fifty feet, and a depth of two hundred feet. The main building and one wing have already been erected, and possess accommodation for about one hundred and fifty patients. To aid in the building of the Hospital, two hundred thousand dollars have been appropriated by the State of Pennsylvania, and three hundred thousand dollars raised by subscription. Accessible by the Darby branch of the Chestnut and Walnut Streets line of cars. The cars on Market Street also pass, at Thirty-fourth Street, within a few squares of the Hospital, and the cars of the West End Railroad from Fairmount Park convey passengers to the immediate vicinity.

Naval Asylum. The United States Naval Asylum, on Gray's Ferry Road, at Bainbridge Street, occupies a plot of ground about twenty-five acres in extent. The principal building is of marble, three hundred and eighty feet in length, and has accommodations for three hundred persons. The grounds are beautifully laid out, and contain, besides the main building, commodious residences for the governor of the Asylum and for the surgeon. The Pine Street cars (Gray's Ferry branch) pass the Asylum.

Pennsylvania Hospital, the oldest and most celebrated of the Hospitals of the city, was founded in 1750. It is located on the square bounded by Eighth, Ninth, Spruce, and Pine Streets, fronting upon Pine, the principal entrance being on Eighth Street. The building has an entire front of two hundred and seventy-eight feet, composed of the main building, sixty-four feet in width, which is connected by wards, eighty feet in extent, with the two wings each twenty-seven feet front. The grounds are tastefully laid out and contain a statue of William Penn, presented to the institution by one of his descendants. The

THE PENNSYLVANIA HOSPITAL.

Hospital is reached from the northern section of the city by the **Sixth Street** cars and the Tenth Street cars, both of which pass, at Spruce Street, within two squares, and also by the cars of the Union line, which pass at Seventh and Spruce Streets, one square distant. From the west the Spruce Street cars pass the grounds, and from the southern section of the city the Eighth Street cars pass the entrance, and the cars of the Union line pass the grounds on Ninth Street.

Pennsylvania Hospital for the Insane, popularly known as "Kirkbride's Lunatic Asylum," is situated north of Market Street and west of Forty-third. It consists of two departments, "male" and "female," capable of accommodating two hundred and fifty patients each. The main buildings of the two departments are similar in construction, three stories in height, with a front range of nearly four hundred and fifty feet, and stand on a plot of ground over one hundred acres in extent. The Hospital is reached by the Market Street cars, Haddington branch.

Philadelphia Hospital, a branch of the Blockley Almshouse, is among the oldest institutions of the kind in the country. The Insane Department of this Hospital contains over a thousand inmates. See BLOCKLEY ALMSHOUSE.

St. Joseph's Hospital, under the care of the Sisters of Charity, is situated on Girard Avenue, on grounds extending from Sixteenth to Seventeenth Streets. The building is a four-story brick structure with a wing, and possesses accommodations for about two hundred and fifty patients. Accessible by the Fourth and Eighth Streets cars (Girard Avenue branch), which pass the door, by the cars on Sixteenth Street, and by the various lines which connect with these routes by *exchange tickets*.

Wills Hospital for Diseases of the Eye is situated on Race Street, opposite Logan Square, between Eighteenth and Nineteenth Streets. It was founded by bequest of James Wills, and opened for patients in 1834. The building is eighty feet long by fifty feet in depth, with pavilion wards, recently erected, ninety feet long. Skillful surgeons attend daily at the Hospital, the operations being free of charge. Accessible from the east by the Vine Street cars and the Arch Street cars, both of which pass, at Eighteenth Street, about two squares distant; from the north by the Seventeenth Street cars, which pass, at Race Street, within two squares; from Fairmount by the Race Street cars, which pass the Hospital, and the Arch Street cars, which pass at Nineteenth Street, one square distant; and from the south by the Nineteenth Street cars, which pass at Race Street, near the building. Other lines connect with these by *exchange tickets* (price nine cents), making the locality easily accessible from all sections.

HOTELS.

American Hotel, 517 Chestnut Street, is reached from the Kensington Depot by the cars running down Sixth Street, which pass at Chestnut Street within a few doors; from the depots at West Philadelphia by the cars down Chestnut Street; and from the Baltimore Depot by the cars of the Union line, which pass at Ninth and Chestnut Streets, three squares distant.

Bingham House, at the corner of Eleventh and Market Streets, is reached from the Kensington Depot by the Sixth Street cars, which connect with the cars on Market Street by *exchange tickets* (price nine cents); from Fairmount by the Arch Street cars, which pass at Eleventh Street, one square distant; from West Philadelphia by the Market Street cars, which pass the door of the hotel, and by the Chestnut Street cars, which pass at Eleventh Street, one square distant; and from the Baltimore Depot by the Fifteenth Street cars, which connect with the Market Street line by *exchange tickets* (price nine cents), and by the cars of the Union line, which pass at Ninth and Market Streets, two squares distant; from the Delaware River the Market Street cars pass the door, and the cars on Walnut Street pass at Eleventh Street, two squares distant.

Colonnade Hotel, at Fifteenth and Chestnut Streets, is reached from the northern sections of the city by the cars going south, which, with the exception of the Union line, connect by *exchange tickets* (price nine cents) with the Market Street cars, and thus convey passengers to Fifteenth and Market Streets, one square distant; from the east the Walnut Street cars also pass at Fifteenth, one square distant; from West Philadelphia the Chestnut Street cars pass the door; from the Baltimore Depot the Fifteenth Street cars also pass the door at Chestnut Street.

Continental Hotel, at Ninth and Chestnut Streets, is reached from the Kensington Depot by the Sixth Street cars, which pass at Chestnut Street, three squares distant; and from the northern sections of the city generally by the cars of the Union line, which convey passengers to Seventh and Chestnut Streets, two squares distant; from the northwest the Ridge Avenue cars, and from Fairmount the Arch Street cars, both pass at Ninth and Arch Streets, two squares distant; from West Philadelphia the Chestnut Street cars pass the hotel; and from the Baltimore Depot the cars of the Union line convey passengers to the door; from the south the Eighth Street cars pass at Chestnut Street, one square distant; and from the Delaware River the Market Street and Walnut Street cars both pass at Ninth Street, one square away.

Girard House is situated on Chestnut Street, near Ninth, directly opposite to the Continental Hotel. For means of reaching the Girard House, see CONTINENTAL HOTEL.

Guy's Hotel, on the European plan, at Seventh and Chestnut Streets, is reached from the Kensington Depot by the Sixth Street cars, which pass at Sixth and Chestnut Streets, one square distant; and from the northern sections of the city generally by the cars of the Union line, which pass the hotel at Seventh and Chestnut Streets; from the northwest the Ridge Avenue cars, and from Fairmount the Arch Street cars, both pass at Seventh and Arch Streets, two squares distant; and from West Philadelphia the Market Street cars pass at Seventh Street, within one square, and the Chestnut Street cars pass the door; from the Baltimore Depot the cars of the Union line pass at Ninth and

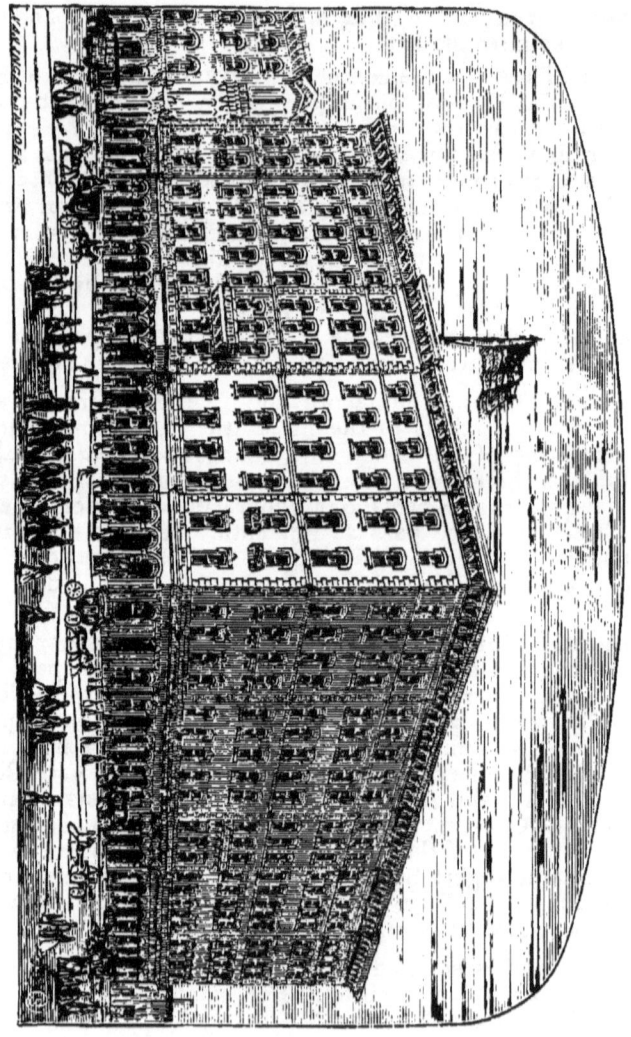

THE CONTINENTAL HOTEL.

Chestnut Streets, two squares distant; and from the south the cars on Eighth Street pass at Chestnut, one square distant; from the Delaware River the Walnut Street cars and the Market Street cars both pass at Seventh Street, one square distant.

LaPierre House, on the west side of Broad Street, below Chestnut Street, is reached from the Kensington Depot by the Sixth Street cars, which connect by *exchange tickets* (price nine cents) with the Walnut Street line, and thus convey passengers to Broad and Walnut Streets, within one square; from the West Philadelphia Depots by the Market Street and Chestnut Street cars, both of which pass at Chestnut Street, within one square; from the Baltimore Depot by the Fifteenth Street cars, which pass at Chestnut Street, one square distant; and from the east by the Market Street and Walnut Street cars, both of which pass at Broad Street, about one square distant.

Merchant's Hotel, situated on Fourth Street, between Market and Arch Streets, is reached from the Kensington Depot by the Sixth Street cars, which pass at Sixth and Arch Streets, two squares distant; from the northwestern section of the city by the Ridge Avenue cars, and from Fairmount by the Arch Street cars, both of which pass at Arch Street, within one square; and from the West Philadelphia Depots by the Market Street cars and the Chestnut Street cars, which pass at Fourth Street, within two squares; from the Baltimore Depot the Fifteenth Street cars connect by *exchange tickets* (price nine cents) with the Market or Arch Street cars, and thus convey passengers within one square of the hotel.

St. Cloud Hotel, at 709 Arch Street, is accessible from the Kensington Depot by the Sixth Street cars, which pass at Arch Street, one square distant; and from the northern sections of the city generally by the cars of the Union line, which pass at Seventh and Arch Streets, within a few doors; the Ridge Avenue cars from the northwest and the Arch Street cars from Fairmount pass the door; and from the West Philadelphia depots the Market Street cars convey passengers to Seventh and Market Streets, one square distant; from the Baltimore Depot the cars of the Union line pass at Ninth and Arch Streets, within two squares; and from the southern section of the city the Eighth Street cars pass at Arch Street, within one square of the hotel.

St. Elmo Hotel, 319 Arch Street, within four squares of the St. Cloud, is reached from different sections of the city by the same lines that convey visitors to that hotel. See ST. CLOUD HOTEL.

St. George Hotel, at the corner of Broad and Walnut Streets, one square from the LaPierre House, is reached from the different sections of the city by the same routes that convey passengers to that hotel. See LAPIERRE HOUSE.

St. Stephen's Hotel, situated on Chestnut Street, between Tenth and Eleventh Streets, is reached from the Kensington Depot by the Sixth Street cars, which convey passengers to Sixth and Chestnut Streets, about four squares distant, and from the northern sections of the city generally by the cars of the Union line, which pass at Seventh and Chestnut Streets, three squares distant; from the West Philadelphia Depots the Market Street cars pass at Eleventh and Market, one square distant, and the Chestnut Street cars pass the door; from the Baltimore Depot the cars of the Union line pass at Ninth and Chestnut Streets, within two squares; and from the depots and ferries on the Delaware River, the Market Street cars and the Walnut Street cars both pass at Eleventh Street, one square distant.

Washington Hotel, at 711 Chestnut Street, above Seventh Street, is a few doors from Guy's Hotel. For means of conveyance to this house, see GUY'S HOTEL.

West End Hotel, a new house on Chestnut Street, below Sixteenth Street, a few doors from the Colonnade. For means of reaching this house, see COLONNADE HOTEL.

INDEPENDENCE HALL.

Little need be said of Independence Hall, for it is known wherever America herself is known, and its history is a familiar one to every schoolboy. Commenced in 1729, and completed in 1735, the State-House is most intimately associated in the American mind with the date 1776. In the east room of the main building (Independence Hall proper) the second Continental Congress met, and there, on the 4th of July, 1776, the Declaration of Independence was adopted, and from the steps leading into Independence Square, then the State-House Yard, it was read to the multitude assembled by the joyful pealing of the bell overhead,—the same bell which now, cracked and useless, but with its grand, prophetic motto still intact, rests in state in the building. And in Congress Hall, in the second story, Washington delivered his farewell address.

Independence Hall is preserved as befits the glorious deed that was done in it. The furniture is the same as that used by Congress; portraits of our country's heroes crowd the walls, and relics of our early history are everywhere. The building stands on the south side of Chestnut Street, between Fifth and Sixth. The three isolated buildings which stood here in 1776 are now connected, others having been built in the spaces between them, and the entire square is now used for court-rooms and offices connected with them, and has a local reputation as "State-House Row."

Visitors are admitted to Independence Hall between 9 A.M. and 4 P.M. daily. An interesting museum of articles connected with American history has been established in an adjoining room, which contains much to attract the attention of the patriotic visitor.

The wide sidewalk in front of State-House Row is paved with slate, which forms an admirable pavement, and is ornamented with trees. Two drinking-fountains represent one of Philadelphia's noblest charities, and a statue of Washington guards the place whose memory is so inseparably linked with his own.

Independence Hall is reached from the northern and northwestern sections of the city by the cars on Fourth and on Sixth Streets (stopping at Chestnut Street); by the cars of the Union line, passing at Seventh

and Chestnut Streets, one square distant; by the Green Street cars, which pass at Fourth and Chestnut, one square distant; and by the Ridge Avenue cars, which pass at Sixth and Arch Streets, two squares distant. From the west the Arch Street cars pass at Sixth and Arch Streets, two squares distant; the Market Street cars, at Sixth and Market, one square distant; the Chestnut Street cars pass the door, and the Spruce Street cars pass at Sixth and Spruce, two squares distant. From the south the Fifth Street cars pass at Chestnut, near the Hall, and the Eighth Street cars two squares distant.

Independence Square. See PUBLIC SQUARES.

Jefferson Medical College. See MEDICAL SCHOOLS.

LEAGUE ISLAND NAVY-YARD.

LEAGUE ISLAND, to which the navy-yard of the United States in Philadelphia has recently been transferred, is situated at the junction of the Delaware and Schuylkill Rivers, at the extreme southern end of Broad Street, and about seven miles from the new City Hall, at Broad and Market Streets. The Island has an area of nearly one thousand acres, and is separated from the mainland by a narrow back channel which extends from the Delaware River to the Schyulkill, near the mouth of the latter. It was presented to the United States Government by the city of Philadelphia in 1862, since which time improvements have been slowly carried forward and several large workshops erected. No public conveyance runs to the Island, but the drive on Broad Street leads to the main entrance to the Yard.

Lemon Hill. See FAIRMOUNT PARK.

LIBRARIES.

The following are the principal public libraries in the city:

Apprentices' Library, at Fifth and Arch Streets, a *free* library, established in 1820, "for the use of apprentices and other young persons, without charge of any kind for the use of books." The Library is divided into two departments, one for boys, containing about fifteen thousand volumes, and one for girls, containing about eight thousand five hundred volumes. A reading-room has also recently been established.

The Arch Street cars, the Ridge Avenue cars, and the Fifth Street cars all pass the Library.

Athenæum Library and Reading-room is situated on Sixth Street, below Walnut, at the corner of Adelphi Street. The building is of brown stone, erected about 1846, and is remarkable for its chaste and beautiful style of architecture.

Mercantile Library, the largest and most popular of the libraries of the city, is located on Tenth Street, between Market and Chestnut Streets. The building is a large, roomy structure, well fitted up for its purposes, and affords ample accommodations for its numerous patrons. The Library has about one hundred and thirty thousand volumes, and

THE MERCANTILE LIBRARY.

numerous periodical publications, American and foreign. Attached are rooms for correspondence, reading, etc., and a chess-room for the use of members. The rooms are open daily until 10 P.M. The Tenth Street cars pass the Library, and the Chestnut Street and Market Street cars pass at Tenth, a half-square distant.

Philadelphia Library, on the northeast corner of Fifth and Library Streets, is the oldest institution of the kind in Philadelphia, having been founded in 1731, mainly through the influence of Dr. Franklin. It was removed to its present location in 1790. This library is particularly rich in classic and standard works, and is much frequented by those engaged in scholarly pursuits. Connected with the Philadelphia Library is the Loganian Library, a bequest of Mr. James Logan, once chief-justice of the Province of Pennsylvania. In 1791 the Loganian Library was placed in charge of the Philadelphia Library Company. These combined libraries contain about one hundred thousand volumes. The rooms are open to visitors from 9 A.M. to 5 P.M. daily, Sundays and holidays excepted.

Ridgway Library. The building of the Ridgway Library occupies the plat of ground extending from Broad to Thirteenth, and from Carpenter to Christian Streets. It is a granite structure, two hundred and twenty feet long by one hundred and five feet deep, and was erected by will of the late Dr. James Rush, and named in honor of his wife, a daughter of Jacob Ridgway, once a wealthy merchant of Philadelphia. By the terms of the will the control of the Library may pass to the Philadelphia Library Company, but, if not accepted by the share-holders, it will be opened as a free library. The Thirteenth Street cars pass the building.

MASONIC TEMPLE.

The Masonic order in the city is very powerful, numbering some seventy-five lodges, the most of whom hold their meetings in the new Masonic Temple, at the northeast corner of Broad and Filbert Streets, above Market. This magnificent structure, having a front of one hundred and fifty feet on Broad Street, with a depth of two hundred and forty-five feet on Filbert, and a height of ninety-five feet, is claimed to be the finest building belonging to this order in the world. It is built of granite, in the Norman style of architecture, exceedingly elaborate, and displays on the Broad Street front two towers, the top of the highest being two hundred and fifty feet from the pavement. The interior arrangement and finish of the structure is quite in harmony with the magnificent exterior, the Temple having cost in its erection and finish one million three hundred thousand dollars. Visitors are admitted on Thursdays of each week, upon introduction by a member of the order.

MEDICAL SCHOOLS.

THE **College of Physicians,** situated at the northeast corner of Thirteenth and Locust Streets, is an organization composed of physicians, having for its object the consideration of matters pertaining to their profession. The College building contains a valuable medical library **and a pathological museum.** The cars on Thirteenth Street pass the

NEW MASONIC TEMPLE.

building from the north; the Walnut Street cars, from the east, pass at Thirteenth, a few doors distant; from the west the Chestnut Street cars pass at Thirteenth Street, within two squares, and the Spruce Street, at Thirteenth, pass within one square. The College is reached from the south by the Eleventh Street and the Fifteenth Street cars, each passing at Locust Street, two squares distant.

Dental Colleges. The two Dental Schools of Philadelphia, called the PENNSYLVANIA COLLEGE OF DENTAL SURGERY and the PHILADELPHIA DENTAL COLLEGE, are situated, respectively, on the southeast and northwest corners of Tenth and Arch Streets. They are reached from the northern section of the city by the cars on Tenth Street and by the Ridge Avenue cars, both of which pass the Colleges; from the west by the cars on Race Street, which pass at Tenth Street, one square distant; by the Arch Street cars, which pass the buildings; and by the Market Street cars, which pass at Tenth Street, one square distant. From the south the Eleventh Street cars pass at Arch, one square distant, and the cars of the Union line pass at Ninth and Arch Streets, within one square.

Hahnemann Medical College (Homœopathic) is situated on Filbert Street, between Eleventh and Twelfth Streets. It is accessible from the northern section of the city by the cars on Twelfth Street, which pass at Filbert, within a square; by the cars on Tenth Street, which pass at Filbert Street, within two squares, and by the cars on Thirteenth Street, which also pass at Filbert, within two squares. From the northwest the Ridge Avenue cars pass at Tenth and Arch Streets, about two squares distant. From both the east and west the cars on Arch Street and Market Street pass at Eleventh Street, within one square, and the Race Street cars and Chestnut Street cars, also at Eleventh Street, pass about two squares distant. From the south the Eleventh Street cars pass near the building, and the cars of the Union line pass at Ninth and Filbert Streets, about two squares distant.

Jefferson Medical College, one of the most celebrated Medical Schools in the country, is situated on Tenth Street, between Chestnut and Walnut Streets. It is reached from the north by the Tenth Street cars, which pass the door; from the west by the Chestnut Street cars, which pass at Tenth, within one square, and by the Market Street cars and the Spruce Street cars, which pass at Tenth, within two squares; from the south by the Eleventh Street cars and the cars of the Union line, both of which pass at Locust Street, one square distant. From the east the Walnut Street cars pass at Tenth Street, within one square.

Philadelphia College of Pharmacy, situated on Tenth Street, between Race and Arch Streets, is reached from the northern section of the city by the Tenth Street cars and by the Ridge Avenue cars, both of which pass the door. From the west the Race Street cars and the cars on Arch Street pass at Tenth Street, within a square, and from the south the Eleventh Street cars and the cars of the Union line, on Ninth Street, pass at Cherry Street, about a square distant. From the east the Arch Street cars pass at Tenth Street, within a square, and the Vine Street cars pass at Tenth, about a square distant.

University of Pennsylvania, Medical Department, situated at the corner of Thirty-fourth and Locust Streets, is an elegant greenstone structure, containing accommodations for six hundred students. This new building was opened for instruction in October, 1874, the school having been in existence at that time for more than one hundred years. Ample appliances are at the command of the faculty for instruction in the various branches of a medical education, besides which clinical lectures at the University Hospital, near at hand, are available to the students. The cars of the Chestnut and Walnut Streets road (Darby branch) pass the College.

Women's Medical College, corner of North College Avenue and Twenty-first Street, was established for the purpose of granting to women a thorough medical education. It was founded in 1849, and was at that time the only medical school for women in the world. The new building, a neat brick structure, was opened in 1875.

MILITARY ESTABLISHMENTS.

First City Troop, officially known as the "First Troop Philadelphia City Cavalry," is distinguished as the oldest cavalry company in the United States, having been formed in 1774. The armory of the Troop, situated on Twenty-first Street, between Market and Chestnut Streets, is an imposing brick and stone structure, having a front of sixty-six feet by one hundred and eighty-eight feet by one hundred and eighty-eight feet in depth. It was enlarged to its present dimensions in 1874, and dedicated on the 17th of November of that year, being the one hundredth anniversary of the organization.

Frankford Arsenal, or Bridesburg Arsenal, a Government institution, under command of the War Department, is situated on grounds extending to the Delaware River, at the mouth of Frankford Creek. The grounds, some sixty acres in extent, are handsomely laid out, and contain extensive appliances for the manufacture of the *materiel* of war. The Bridesburg branch of the Second and Third Streets Railroad line conveys passengers to the Arsenal.

Gray Reserves, the First Regiment National Guards, have their headquarters at the City Armory, on the east side of Broad Street, below Race Street.

Keystone Battery. This artillery company has its armory on Broad Street, near Mount Vernon Street. The Fifteenth Street cars pass at Mount Vernon, near the armory, and the Eighth Street cars up Fairmount Avenue convey passengers to within a few doors of the building.

National Guards, now designated as the Second Regiment Pennsylvania National Guards, have their armory on the south side of Race Street, below Sixth. The building is of brick, three stories in height, with an observatory.

Schuylkill Arsenal, a Government institution, on Gray's Ferry Road, at Washington Street, is an establishment for the manufacture and storage of military clothing, of which enormous quantities are turned out every year. The products include everything connected with the uniform of the soldier and the principal articles of camp equipage. As many as a thousand women are sometimes employed at the Arsenal. The establishment is reached by the Pine Street cars (Gray's Ferry branch), which pass the entrance.

Washington Grays, an artillery corps, at present acting as infantry, have their armory on Lardner Street, west of Broad, above Spruce, at the rear of Horticultural Hall.

MINT.

The Philadelphia Mint, the oldest and most celebrated of the institutions of the kind in the United States, is located on Chestnut Street,

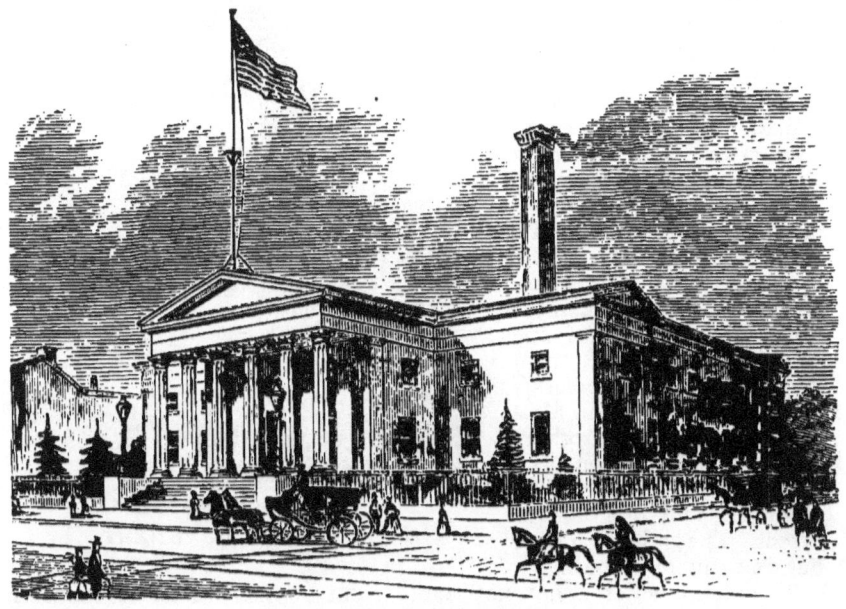

UNITED STATES MINT.

between Thirteenth and Broad. This building was erected in 1829, pursuant to an act of Congress enlarging the operations of the government coining, and supplementary to the act creating the Mint, which was passed in 1792. The structure is of the Ionic order, copied from a temple at Athens. It is of brick, faced with marble ashlar.

Visitors are admitted before twelve o'clock, every day except Saturday and Sunday; and the beautiful and delicate operations and contrivances for coining, as well as the extensive numismatic cabinet, are well worth seeing.

The cars on Thirteenth and Fifteenth Streets pass at Chestnut Street, near the Mint, and the Chestnut Street cars pass the door.

PENN TREATY MONUMENT.

This monument marks the site of the great elm-tree under which William Penn made his famous treaty with the Indians at Shackamaxon (now Kensington),—a name still preserved in the nomenclature of the streets in that vicinity. The silent witness of "the only treaty ever ratified without an oath, and the only one never broken," stood for more than a century. It was a favorite resort in summer time; the citizens sat under its branches, and whole congregations worshiped in its shade; but in 1810 it was blown down, and nothing now remains to mark the place where it stood but an insignificant monument, which none but a sharp eye can discover. It stands on the east side of Beach Street, a few steps north of Hanover (which is marked Columbia Street on most maps). The visitor who has imbibed the popular fallacy that the streets of Philadelphia are straight, and cross each other at right angles, has only to visit Kensington to be thoroughly and permanently cured of that idea. If he can make his way, unassisted, from any business centre to the site of the famous Treaty Tree, without becoming hopelessly bewildered, he will do for a backwoodsman. All others should take the Second and Third Street cars (Richmond branch) to Hanover Street. They will then have but one square to walk.

PENN TREATY MONUMENT.

The stone, which is not noticeable from across the street, stands in an inclosure just large enough to hold it, in the midst of stone and lumber yards, and in the shade of a tall elm which may possibly be a lineal descendant of the one whose site it shades.

POST-OFFICE.

The present building of the United States Post-Office is located on Chestnut Street, below Fifth. The front is of Pennsylvania marble, and with its mansard roof the building presents a fine appearance. The second floor is occupied in part by the United States courts. A new post-office is now in course of construction at Ninth and Chestnut Streets. See CUSTOM-HOUSE, page 52.

MOYAMENSING PRISON.

PRISONS.

Eastern Penitentiary of Pennsylvania, popularly known as "Cherry Hill Prison," a State institution, is situated on Fairmount Avenue, at Twenty-second Street, having a front on Fairmount Avenue of six hundred and seventy feet.

The grounds connected with this prison embrace about eleven acres nearly all of which space is covered with buildings, the whole being surrounded with a stone wall thirty feet high. The plan of the buildings may be compared to a star with seven rays, there being a central hall with seven corridors running from it, so arranged that the warden, sitting in the centre, has the whole length of each corridor under his eye.

The "separate" (*not* solitary) system of confinement is adopted here, but is modified to the extent of confining two prisoners in each of the larger cells whenever the crowded state of the prison renders it necessary. Each prisoner is furnished with work enough to keep him moderately busy, and is permitted to earn money for himself by overwork. He is allowed to see and converse with the chaplain, prison-inspectors, and other officials, and an occasional visitor, but not with any of his fellow-prisoners. The advantages claimed for this system are that convicts have leisure and opportunity for reflection, and for the formation of steady and correct habits, and are not in danger, when set free, of meeting other prisoners who can identify them, and thus obtain a fearful influence over them. Visitors to the Eastern Penitentiary will take the Green and Coates Streets cars (running out Eighth Street), or the yellow cars of the Union line, running out Ninth and up Spring Garden.

House of Refuge, an institution for "the employment of the idle, instruction of the ignorant, and reformation of the depraved," is located on the square bounded by Twenty-second, Twenty-third, Parrish, and Poplar Streets. The managers are a corporate body, and are empowered to receive youths of both sexes committed to their care by the courts.

The institution is reached by the cars of the Union line (Fairmount branch) and by the Girard Avenue branch of the Fourth and Eighth Streets line. Visitors are admitted every afternoon, except Saturday and Sunday, on presentation of tickets, which may be procured of the managers or at the *Public Ledger* office.

Moyamensing Prison, the County Prison of Philadelphia, is situated at Tenth Street and Passyunk Avenue. It is a massive granite structure, consisting of a central building and two wings, flanked with octagonal towers, and contains four hundred cells for males and one hundred cells for female prisoners.

Visitors to the Prison take the cars on Tenth or on Twelfth Street, or the cars of the Union line going south, all of which convey passengers to the immediate vicinity. Visitors' permits are obtained at the Mayor's office, at Fifth and Chestnut Streets.

PUBLIC SQUARES.

Franklin Square, one of the four principal public Squares of the city, extends from Vine Street on the north to Race Street on the

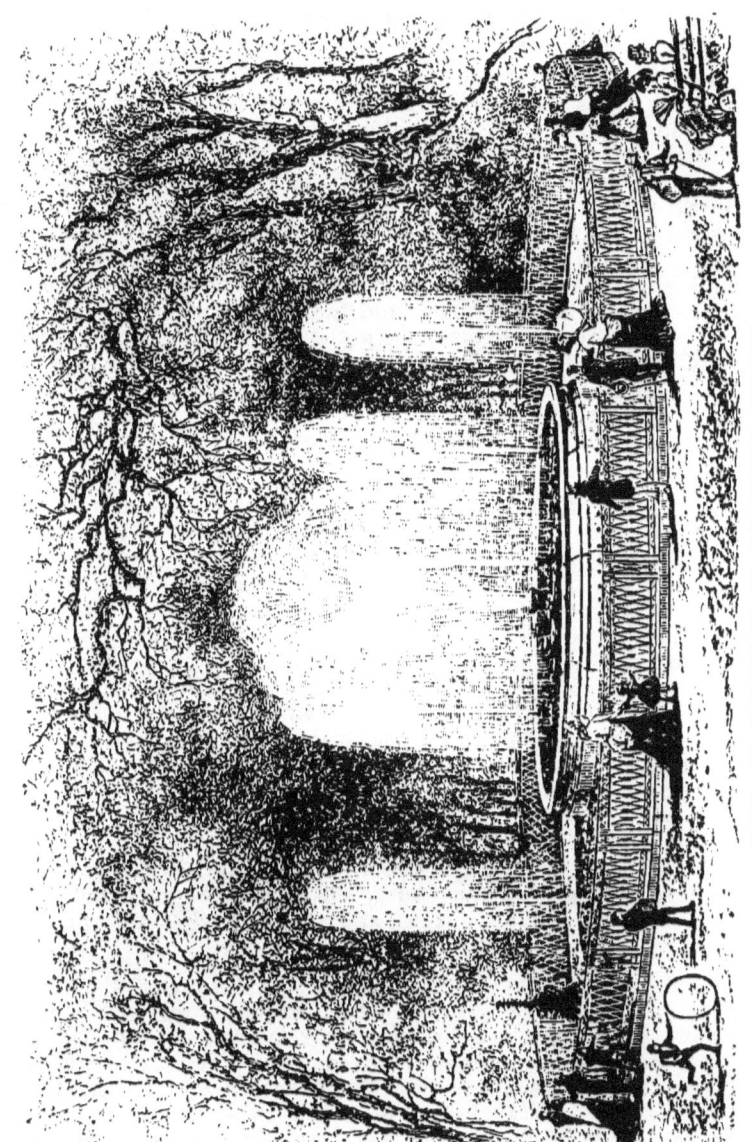

VIEW OF FOUNTAIN IN FRANKLIN SQUARE.

south, and from Sixth Street on the east to Franklin Street on the west, covering an area of over seven acres. It is filled with fine shade-trees, and in its centre is a beautiful fountain. Franklin Square is reached from the northern and northwestern sections of the city by the cars on Sixth Street, and by the cars of the Union line, both of which pass the Square; also by the Ridge Avenue cars, which, at Tenth and Vine, pass two squares distant, and the Green Street cars, which pass at Fourth and Vine Streets, two squares distant. From the west, the Callowhill Street cars pass at Seventh Street, one square distant, the Race Street cars pass the Square, and the Arch Street cars at Seventh Street pass one square distant; from the southern and southeastern sections of the city, the cars of the Union line pass at Ninth and Race, two squares distant, the Eighth Street cars pass at Race Sreet, within one square, and the Vine Street cars pass the Square. Franklin Square (formerly called *Northeast Square*) is one of the five Squares originally dedicated to the city by William Penn.

Independence Square, so called in grateful remembrance that in it Liberty was first proclaimed to the people, extends from Chestnut Street on the north to Walnut Street on the south, and from Fifth Street on the east to Sixth Street on the west. It is partly occupied by INDEPENDENCE HALL (q. v.) and adjoining buildings—including the rooms of the Philosophical Society. Independence Square is reached from the northern and northwestern sections of the city by the cars on Fourth Street, which pass at Fourth and Chestnut Streets, one square distant; by the cars of the Union line, which, at Seventh and Chestnut Streets, pass within one square; by the Green Street cars, which also pass Fourth and Chestnut, and by the Ridge Avenue cars, which, at Sixth and Arch Streets, pass two squares distant; from the west, the Arch Street cars pass at Sixth Street, two squares distant; the Market Street cars pass at Sixth Street, one square distant; the Chestnut Street cars pass the Square at Sixth Street, and the Spruce Street cars pass at Sixth, one square distant; from the south, the Eighth Street cars pass at Walnut Street, two squares distant, and the Fifth Street cars pass the Square.

Logan Square, originally called *Northwest Square*, and under this name ceded to the city by William Penn, extends from Vine Street on the north to Race Street on the south, and westward from Eighteenth Street, embracing an area of over seven acres. It is accessible from the northern part of the city by the Seventeenth Street cars, and by the lines which cross and exchange with the Seventeenth Street line; from the west by the Callowhill Street cars, which pass at Nineteenth Street, one square distant; by the Race Street cars, which pass the Square; by the Arch Street cars, which pass at Nineteenth Street, one square distant, and by the Market Street cars, which pass at Nineteenth Street, two squares distant; from the south, the Nineteenth Street cars pass the Square, and the Sixteenth Street cars pass at Race Street, two squares distant; from the east, the Market Street cars pass, two squares distant, at Eighteenth Street; the Arch Street cars, at Eighteenth, one square distant; the Vine Street cars pass the Square, and the Callow-

VIEW AT LOGAN SQUARE.

hill Street cars pass at Nineteenth Street, one square distant. Other lines of cars, exchanging with these several lines, render Logan Square easy of access from all parts of the city.

Rittenhouse Square, originally called *Southwest Square*, extends from Walnut Street on the north to Locust Street on the south, and from Eighteenth Street westward, embracing an area of six acres. It is a popular place of resort, especially for children, being densely shaded by large trees and handsomely ornamented with fountains.

Rittenhouse Square is reached from the northern section of the city by the cars on Seventeenth Street, which pass one square distant, at Seventeenth and Walnut Streets; and from Fairmount by the Spruce Street cars, which pass within a square, at Spruce and Nineteenth Streets. From the east the Market Street cars pass at Nineteenth and Market Streets, two squares distant, the Walnut Street cars pass the Square, and the Pine Street cars pass at Nineteenth Street within two squares. From the west the Market Street cars pass at Nineteenth and Market, two squares distant; the Chestnut Street cars, at Nineteenth, pass one square distant, and the Spruce Street cars, at Nineteenth, within a square. From the south the cars on Nineteenth Street pass the Square. Rittenhouse Square is surrounded by elegant residences.

Washington Square, the *Southeast Square* of Penn's time, is located at Sixth and Walnut Streets (near Independence Square, q. v.), extending from Walnut Street on the north to Locust Street on the south, and from Sixth Street westward, containing an area of over six acres. It is covered by a luxuriant growth of shade-trees. Washington Square is reached from the northern section of the city by the Sixth Street cars, which pass the Square on the east side, and by the cars of the Union line, which pass it on the west side. The cars on Fourth Street pass at Fourth and Walnut, two squares distant; and the Green Street cars (Walnut Street branch) pass the Square on Walnut Street. From the west the Market Street cars pass at Seventh Street, two squares distant, the Chestnut Street cars pass at Seventh, one square distant, and the Spruce Street cars from Fairmount and Gray's Ferry pass at Seventh Street within a square. From the south the cars of the Union line pass at Ninth and Walnut Streets, within two squares; the Eighth Street cars pass at Eighth and Walnut, within one square, and the Fifth Street cars pass at Fifth and Walnut, one square distant. Washington Square was once a burial-place, a "Potter's Field."

RAILROAD DEPOTS.

The **Baltimore Depot**—that is, the Depot of the Philadelphia, Wilmington and Baltimore Railroad—is situated on South Broad Street, at Washington Avenue, and is reached by the cars on Thirteenth Street, which convey passengers to the entrance, by the cars on Twelfth Street, which pass at Carpenter Street two squares distant, and by the cars of the Union line going southward, which pass the building. Other lines running east and west *exchange* with the Thirteenth Street cars (fare nine cents), and render the Depot accessible from all sections of the city.

VINE STREET FERRY, TERMINUS OF THE CAMDEN AND ATLANTIC RAILROAD.

Camden and Atlantic Railroad Depot. The Philadelphia Depot of the Camden and Atlantic Railroad to Atlantic City is located at Vine Street Wharf, on the Delaware River, and connects by ferry with the Depot at Camden. The Callowhill Street Railroad is the only line that conveys passengers direct to the Depot, but the railways running north and south connect by *exchange tickets* (price nine cents) with the Callowhill Street line, and thus render the Depot easily accessible from all parts of the city.

North Pennsylvania Railroad. The Depot of the North Pennsylvania Railroad is situated at Berks and America Streets, in the northern section of the city, and is reached by the Third Street cars, by the Fifth Street cars, and by the cars of the Union line (Richmond branch), all of which convey passengers to the immediate vicinity of the Depot. Lines of cars running east and west connect with the Third Street and Fifth Street lines by *exchange tickets* (price nine cents). The time required to reach the Depot from Chestnut Street is about thirty minutes.

Pennsylvania Railroad Depots. The principal Depot of the Pennsylvania Railroad is situated at Thirty-second and Market Streets, and is reached by the Market Street cars, and by the Fairmount Park branch of the Walnut Street cars, both of which convey passengers to the Depot. Lines running north and south connect by *exchange tickets* (price nine cents) with these lines. The principal trains for the north (New York) and west (Pittsburgh) leave this Depot. THE KENSINGTON DEPOT of the Pennsylvania Railroad is situated in the northern part of the city, at Front and Berks Streets, and is reached by the cars on Fifth Street, on Third Street, and by the Richmond branch of the Union line. Lines of cars crossing Fifth Street from the western section of the city connect by means of *exchange tickets* (price nine cents) with the cars of that line.

Reading Railroad Depot, or principal Depot of the Philadelphia and Reading Railroad, is situated at Broad and Callowhill Streets, and is reached from the east by the cars on Callowhill Street, which pass the Depot, and the cars on Vine Street, which pass at Thirteenth Street, one square distant; from the north by the cars on Thirteenth Street, which pass the building, and the cars on Twelfth Street, which pass at Callowhill, one square distant; from the west by the cars on Callowhill Street, which pass the building, and from the south by the cars on Fifteenth Street, which pass at Callowhill Street, one square distant. Various lines of cars from different sections of the city cross these several lines and connect with them by *exchange tickets* (price nine cents). THE GERMANTOWN DEPOT, or Depot of the Germantown and Norristown division of the Philadelphia and Reading Railroad, is situated at Ninth and Green Streets, and is reached from the north by the cars on Tenth Street, which pass at Green Street, one square distant, and by the cars of the Union line (Richmond branch), which pass at Green Street, about one square away; from the west by the Green Street cars, which pass the depot, and the cars of the Union line, which pass near the Depot at Ninth and Wallace Streets; from the south by the cars of the Union line, which pass at Ninth and Spring Garden Streets, within one

PENNSYLVANIA INSURANCE AND TRUST CO'S BUILDING.

square, and the Eighth Street cars, which pass at Green Street within one square, and from all sections of the city by the various lines which connect by *exchange tickets* (price nine cents) with these routes.

West Chester Depot (of the Philadelphia and West Chester Railroad) is situated at Thirty-first and Chestnut Streets, and is accessible from the eastern and western sections of the city by the Chestnut and Walnut Street cars, which pass the Depot at Thirty-first and Chestnut Streets, and by the Market Street cars, which pass at Thirty-first and Market Streets, one square distant.

West Jersey Railroad to Cape May. Visitors to Cape May or other points on the West Jersey Railroad leave the city at Market Street Wharf, on the Delaware River, by ferry to Camden. From the northern and northwestern sections of the city the ferry is reached by the Second Street cars and the cars of the Union line (Market Street branch); from the western section the Market Street cars run to the ferry, the Race Street cars pass at Second and Market Streets, two squares distant, and the Chestnut Street cars at Second and Chestnut, within three squares. The Ridge Avenue cars and the Arch Street cars also run to Second and Arch Streets, three squares distant.

SAFE DEPOSIT AND TRUST COMPANIES.

Fidelity Insurance, Trust, and Safe Deposit Company is located on Chestnut Street, between Third and Fourth Streets.

Girard Life Annuity and Trust Company is located on the northeast corner of Seventh and Chestnut Streets.

Guarantee Trust and Safe Deposit Company is situated on Chestnut Street, between Third and Fourth Streets, at the corner of Hudson Street. The building is a new and very imposing structure, in the Venetian style of architecture.

Northern Saving Fund Safe Deposit and Trust Company occupy a fine granite building on the corner of Sixth and Spring Garden Streets.

Penn Trust and Safe Deposit Company is located in the building of the Spring Garden Bank, on Spring Garden Street, above Twelfth Street.

Pennsylvania Company for Insurances on Lives and Granting Annuities is located on Chestnut Street, below Fifth. The building is a new and massive structure, built of granite.

Philadelphia Trust, Safe Deposit, and Insurance Company is located on Chestnut Street, above Fourth, in a fine marble building adjoining the Philadelphia Bank.

Provident Life and Trust Company. The building of this Company is located on Fourth Street, below Chestnut. It has a massive iron front, and presents an imposing appearance.

THE SCHUYLKILL RIVER FROM NORTH LAUREL HILL.

SCHUYLKILL RIVER.

Chief among the natural attractions within the environs of the city is the famous Schuylkill River, whose banks from the Fairmount Water-Works northward to the mouth of the romantic Wissahickon present an unbroken panorama of charming landscapes; and no visitor to Philadelphia should consider his visit completed until he has availed himself of the opportunity of a drive through FAIRMOUNT PARK (q. v.),

UP THE SCHUYLKILL FROM COLUMBIA BRIDGE.

which lines the River upon either side, or of an excursion upon the miniature steamers, which during the summer constantly ply upon its placid waters.

Southward from Fairmount to the mouth of the stream, at LEAGUE ISLAND NAVY-YARD (q. v.), the banks of the River are available for business purposes; though up to the present time there has been comparatively little demand for the facilities thus offered. Seven bridges

VIEW OF THE SCHUYLKILL RIVER AND BLOCKLEY ALMSHOUSE.

have been erected over this section of the stream, some of which are fine specimens of that class of architecture, and some noteworthy establishments stand upon the banks. Near the mouth of the River, upon the east bank, is the Girard Point Elevator, owned by the International Steam Navigation Company. The elevator is two hundred feet long by one hundred broad, and possesses a capacity of eight hundred thousand bushels. Six vessels may be loaded with grain at the same time, the twelve elevators having a working capacity of fifty-four thousand bushels per hour. The docks and warehouses of the Red Star line of steamers are also at this point. Farther up the stream, but still outside of the built-up portion of the city, are located the Point Breeze Gas-Works, near which are extensive petroleum refineries, and farther up still are the United States Arsenal (see MILITARY ESTABLISHMENTS) and the Marine Hospital (see HOSPITALS AND ASYLUMS), while nearly opposite the latter, on the west side, is BLOCKLEY ALMSHOUSE (q. v.), with its extensive grounds. From this point to Fairmount both banks of the stream are lined, for much of the distance, with stone-yards, coal-wharves, lumber-docks, etc. Upon the eastern bank, above Market Street Bridge, stand the City Gas-Works, while opposite are the grain depot and extensive stock-yards and abattoir of the Pennsylvania Railroad.

In sharp contrast with these scenes, however, is the appearance of the river course at and above Fairmount. Starting from the wharf in the immediate vicinity of the water-works, the little steamer at the outset passes Lemon Hill, at the foot of which stand several boathouses (see BOAT-CLUBS), and on the summit nestles among the trees the once famous mansion of Robert Morris, the distinguished financier of Revolutionary times. Farther onward, on the right, we pass a bluff, crowned with a tasty summer-house overlooking the River, and beyond a natural grove on the steep hill-side. Opposite we catch a glimpse of the grounds of the ZOOLOGICAL GARDEN (q. v.), while farther up the stream the elegant proportions of the Girard Avenue Bridge (see BRIDGES) arrest the attention. Above this bridge, bluffs and ravines on either bank give variety to a succession of charming landscape views, while the whole prospect is pleasingly diversified by the several bridges which span the stream at intervals. Among the noted places which line the banks of the stream are Mount Pleasant and Rockland Mansion, on the east, both near Columbia Bridge (the former once the property of Benedict Arnold), and farther up, on the same side, the Edgely Bluffs stand out in bold relief. In the middle of the stream is Peters' Island, and on the west side, just above the Belmont Railroad Station, is "Tom Moore's Cottage." Back from the River, on the east side, and near the boundary of South Laurel Hill Cemetery (see CEMETERIES), stands "Strawberry Mansion," now kept as a Park restaurant. But chief among the attractions of the upper Schuylkill is the beautiful Laurel Hill Cemetery, the most celebrated of all the rural burial-places near the city. A short distance above Laurel Hill stands Falls Village,—the terminus of the steamboat route from Fairmount,—beyond which the Schuylkill is joined by its romantic affluent, the WISSAHICKON (q. v.).

STREETS.

Arch Street, though a wide and handsome avenue, has never found its course obstructed by such a tide of travel and traffic as surges through some of the other streets. It has always been eminently "respectable," and a certain air of old-time gentility still invests it; one feels that, in passing from Market to Arch, he has unconsciously stepped back fifty years into the past; the roar and hurry of to-day have given way to the steady-going, quiet ways of the earlier years of the century, and he would scarcely be surprised to see a gentleman in powdered

FRANKLIN'S GRAVE.

wig, knee-breeches, and three-cornered hat descending from any one of the stately dwellings whose uniform brick fronts, green shutters, and marble steps are the representatives of, if not the foundation for, the monotonous Philadelphia which satirical visitors are fond of depicting. The lower part of the street has, indeed, been invaded, to a certain extent, by the bustling life of commerce; but west of Eleventh Street all is quiet, and the street is lined with the dwellings of the merchant princes of the city.

Consequently, we have few points of interest to note here. In our walk up-street, we stop, of course, to look through the iron railing set in the wall of Christ Church burying-ground, at Fifth and Arch, and pay our homage to the grave of Benjamin Franklin; and we cannot fail to notice, as we pass, the ancient Friends' Meeting-House which stands on the south side of the street, between Third and Fourth, surrounded by a yard whose dimensions suggest the good old times of its erection, when land was plenty and taxes light. This meeting-house was built in 1808. It is the successor of one which stood in High Street, and has ever since been one of the principal places of worship of the Quakers in Philadelphia. This denomination, being that to which Penn and his followers belonged, was, naturally, the first to erect a place of worship. "The Great Meeting-House," as it was called, at the corner of Second and High Streets, was erected in 1695, on land bestowed by George Fox, "for truth's and Friends' sake." "Great as it was," says Watson, "it was taken down in 1755, to build greater;" and in 1808 the "street noise of increased population" drove the worshipers to the quiet retreat on Arch Street, where they still find themselves able to worship without disturbance.

A little above Sixth Street we pass the Arch Street Theatre (see AMUSEMENTS), one of the standard places of amusement in the city. Another square westward, we come to the St. Cloud Hotel (see HOTELS), a new and excellent house, and very convenient to the business part of the city. And still farther on we find two other places of amusement,—the Museum, on the corner of Ninth, and Simmons and Slocum's Opera-House, a few doors above Tenth. (See AMUSEMENTS.) On Arch, above Tenth, are the Methodist Book Rooms,—the Mecca of Methodist pilgrims; and at Broad and Arch are the stately churches elsewhere spoken of. The rest of the street is "living-room;" it is filled with the homes of the people, with few exceptions, presenting a remarkable sameness of appearance and size.

Broad Street. This noble avenue has its southern terminus at LEAGUE ISLAND (q. v.), the new navy-yard, at the junction of the Delaware and Schuylkill Rivers.

Crossing the back channel by a draw-bridge, Broad Street extends northward through a low, flat tract of land which is now occupied by truck-farms, and which will require much labor to fit it for building purposes. Two rows of trees have been planted in the drive along this part of the street, and these will in a few years afford three leafy avenues for carriages.

The first building of importance which we notice in going north on this street is the Baltimore Depot (see RAILROAD DEPOTS), at Broad and Prime Strees. Many handsome churches and other structures diversify the street to the north of this depot, but it is impossible to mention all in detail. Near the depot stands the new building of the Ridgway Library (see LIBRARIES), and on the corner of Pine Street we pass the Deaf and Dumb Asylum. (See HOSPITALS AND ASYLUMS.) One square above, we pass the magnificent "Beth-Eden" Baptist Church)see CHURCHES), one of the handsomest on Broad Street, even without the spire, which is still wanting to complete the symmetry of the design.

Now, the places of interest crowd thick and fast upon the visitor's attention. Just above Beth-Eden Church is Horticultural Hall. Next door to Horticultural Hall, and so near to it that on grand festive occasions both buildings are leased and connected by a temporary bridge, is the American Academy of Music, the most capacious opera-house in the United States, while opposite rise the ponderous proportions of the Colosseum and the graceful structure known as the Alhambra. (See AMUSEMENTS AND AUDIENCE HALLS.) Following in regular order after the Academy of Music and on the same side of the street are the St. George Hotel and the UNION LEAGUE (q. v.), and immediately above the latter the Hotel Lafayette (reconstructed from the old Academy of Natural Sciences) and the La Pierre House, a well-known hotel.

We now cross Chestnut Street, glance at the Corinthian porticos of two Presbyterian churches on the east side of Broad Street, one above and the other below Chestnut Street, and in a moment reach the new Public Buildings for law-courts and public offices. (See CITY HALL.)

Near the northwest corner of these buildings is the School of Design for Women, and on the northeast corner of Broad and Filbert Streets the new MASONIC TEMPLE (q. v.) rears its stately head high above the neighboring houses.

Adjoining the Masonic Temple on the north is the Arch Street Methodist Episcopal Church, the handsomest church of this denomination in the city. The intersection of Broad and Arch Streets is, indeed, noteworthy for its churches. The pure white marble of the Methodist Church, on the southeast corner, the rich brown stone of the First Baptist Church, on the northwest corner, and the green syenite of the Lutheran Church, on the southwest corner, present a group of architectural beauty scarcely to be surpassed in any city.

At this point occurs an interruption of the usual magnificent display of Broad Street,—a region of warehouses and lumber-yards, which once threatened to be permanent, but to which the removal of the railroad tracks from Broad Street gave a death-blow: so that we may now hope to see their places occupied before long by structures in keeping with the magnificent plan of the street. Nevertheless, it must be confessed that, at the present writing, Broad Street from Arch to Callowhill is *not* a pleasant thoroughfare. The new Academy of Fine Arts, at Broad and Cherry, will do much for this part of the street.

At Callowhill Street we come to the passenger depot of the Philadelphia and Reading Railroad, and just above it, but on the opposite side of the street, the extensive buildings of the Baldwin Locomotive Works, an establishment which boasts the proud distinction of being the largest, as it is among the oldest, of its kind in the world.

On the southeast corner of Broad and Green Streets stands the Central High School,—a plain but not inelegant brick edifice,—and on the northeast corner a handsome Presbyterian church, built in the Norman style of architecture. Beside this stands the Jewish synagogue Rodef Shalom, a good specimen of the Saracenic style, and a very handsome though very peculiar building. Above this point, the section of Broad

Street extending from Fairmount Avenue to Columbia Avenue, a distance of about a mile, is lined with handsome private residences, and is a favorite drive and promenade. On Sunday afternoons the sidewalks are crowded with promenaders, and the whole presents a scene of life and animation strikingly in contrast with the Sabbath stillness of the rest of the city.

The splendid Episcopal church of the Incarnation, at Broad and Jefferson, and several other fine buildings in the immediate vicinity, close the list of objects of interest on Broad Street for the present. Montgomery Avenue is the northern limit of continuous building on this street just now; but the noble boulevard continues straight as an arrow northward, the houses are fast following it, and it cannot be very many years before it will be crowded with stately buildings all the way to Germantown.

Chestnut Street. The stranger visiting Philadelphia will naturally consider Chestnut Street as the representative of the city. Its noble buildings, its handsome stores, and especially the crowds which at all times throng its sidewalks, induce him to associate the idea of Philadelphia with this single street; and it is this which presents itself to his mind's eye whenever the city is afterwards named in his hearing. Let us in imagination traverse the entire length of the street, and note its objects of interest.

Starting from the Delaware front of the city, at Chestnut Street Wharf, where many river steamers land, we turn our faces westward, pass through the tide of commerce which ever flows along Delaware Avenue, on the river bank, and climb the rather steep grade leading up to Front Street, which still presents a reminder of William Penn's "high and dry bank."

The lofty fronts of wholesale dry-goods houses, which line both sides of the street as far as Third Street, together with the narrow sidewalks, make this portion of it seem narrow and gloomy, though the roadway is of uniform width from end to end. At Second Street we make a diversion to the left, and in a moment stand before the Chamber of Commerce, the new and handsome hall of the Commercial Exchange. This building, which is of brown stone, in the Roman-Gothic style, was built in 1870, on the site of the first Exchange, which was destroyed by fire about a year before, while still in its first youth, and which was the noble successor of what was, in its time, a noble mansion,—the "Slate-Roof House."

Immediately opposite the Chamber of Commerce stands a plain brick building, chiefly conspicuous from its great size and severe simplicity of style. This contains the United States Appraiser's Stores, and is noted as being one of the few really fire-proof buildings in America. Its brick walls are of enormous thickness, and the windows are protected by iron shutters, set in niches so deep that no fire can warp them open. Inside, all is of iron and brick, coated with fire-proof cement where necessary, and so arranged that the entire contents of one room may burn without injuring anything contained in the adjoining apartments.

Retracing our steps to Chestnut Street, we admire the handsome buildings which adorn it between Second and Third Streets.

Third Street is the home of the bankers and brokers. To a certain extent, it is the Wall Street of Philadelphia. On it we find the eminent banking-house of Drexel & Co., and many others.

Again turning to the left, we pass the office of the *Evening Telegraph*, and a few doors below it find the Girard Bank, a venerable but still stately edifice, built 1795-8 for the first United States Bank, and afterwards occupied by the man whose name it bears, and whose memory Philadelphia must ever cherish as that of the most munificent benefactor she has ever had.

Again resuming our way up Chestnut Street, we pass, on the south side, the office of the *Inquirer*, and immediately after, on the north, the Bank of North America, the first bank established in the United States, it having been founded by Congress in 1781, when the credit of the country was very far indeed below par.

The present building is of brown stone, in the Florentine style of architecture. Next above, and separated from the bank only by a narrow alley, is the new building of the Guarantee Trust and Safe Deposit Company, a beautiful structure of pressed brick ornamented with Ohio stone and colored tiles. Its frontage on Chestnut Street is 57 feet, and its depth 198 feet.

Below Fourth Street, and opposite Carpenters' Hall, is the elegant white marble building of the Fidelity Safe Deposit and Insurance Company, which combines a handsome exterior with the most impregnable security that modern science can devise. It is in the Italian style, with a front of Lee marble, and is the largest enterprise of the kind in the country. The CUSTOM-HOUSE (q. v.) stands on the south side of the street, between Fourth and Fifth Streets. Opposite the Custom-House, just above the Philadelphia Bank, a handsome granite building, stands the Farmers' and Mechanics' Bank, an imposing white marble structure. This Bank, one of the oldest institutions of its kind in the city, commenced its existence in 1807, with a capital of $700,000.

Adjoining the Farmers' and Mechanics' Bank, just above, is the building of the Pennsylvania Life Insurance and Trust Company. The front is of Quincy granite, of a massive and imposing style of architecture, well suited to the substantial character of the Company, which is the oldest of its kind in the city, having been established in 1812. Just above the Custom-House is the POST-OFFICE (q. v.), and around the corner, in Fifth Street, the Philadelphia Library. (See LIBRARIES.)

The building of the American Philosophical Society stands opposite the Library. The dream-life into which one unconsciously falls in the alcoves of the Library is rudely broken, as he steps out, by the constant bustle about the Mayor's Office and the Police Headquarters, on the southwest corner of Fifth and Chestnut. This building is at the eastern end of "State-House Row," with INDEPENDENCE HALL (q. v.), standing in the middle of the Row.

On the southwest corner of Sixth and Chestnut the imposing brownstone pile of the *Ledger* building attracts the stranger's eye, and he recognizes it at once as one of the lions of the city. Nearly opposite is the office of the *Evening Bulletin*.

At this point the fashionable promenade **may be said to begin. Bright**

PUBLIC LEDGER BUILDING.

faces and gay costumes throng the sidewalk beyond this, and the street is lined with the tastefully arranged shop-windows for which Philadelphia is noted.

The extensive and elegant front of the old Masonic Temple next attracts attention. It is a very beautiful building, and was once considered the finest of its kind in the United States; but it became too small, and the brethren of the mystic tie accordingly built the new and splendid structure at Broad and Filbert Streets. (See MASONIC TEMPLE.) The old one will probably be devoted to business uses, the handsome stores already in the building showing its fitness for such purposes. At the corner of Eighth Street is the new office of the *Times*, and one block above, the Girard House lifts its stately front, while across the way stands the far-famed Continental. (See HOTELS.)

Diagonally across from the Continental is the site for the new Post-Office, on the north side of Chestnut, above Ninth. It will occupy half the square between Chestnut and Market and Ninth and Tenth. The ground appropriated to its use extends from Chestnut to Market Streets, a distance of 484 feet, and is 175 feet 9 inches in width. The building will cover 425 feet 8 inches on Ninth Street by 150 feet on Chestnut and Market.

On the southwest corner of Ninth and Chestnut stands a group of marble stores which are unsurpassed for substantial beauty in the city. Fine stores, indeed, may be said to be the rule from Ninth to Eleventh, and there are many on either side of these limits.

On the northwest corner of Tenth and Chestnut Streets stands the magnificent granite building of the Mutual Life Insurance Company of New York. It is one of the handsomest structures in the city, and is a fit representative of the enterprise of the great and wealthy corporation that erected it, and whose offices are located within its walls.

"Girard Row," on the north side of Chestnut from Eleventh to Twelfth, contains many elegant stores.

The splendid building containing Bailey & Co.'s jewelry store, on the southeast corner of Twelfth and Chestnut, will excite the admiration of the visitor. This store-room is the largest of its kind in the city. It presents a front of forty-four feet on Chestnut Street by two hundred and forty feet on Twelfth, and its ceiling is twenty-two feet in height. The building was erected by Dr. S. S. White, who occupies all of it, except the first floor.

We next pass the Chestnut Street Theatre and Concert Hall, on the opposite side of the street, and, crossing Thirteenth Street, come to the United States Mint. (See MINT.)

Opposite the Mint is the new building of the Presbyterian Board of Publication. Soon after crossing Broad Street, we pass the elegant building of the Baptist Board of Publication.

Here, on opposite corners of Fifteenth and Chestnut, stand the hall of the Young Men's Christian Association and the Colonnade Hotel. Farther on are the Reform Club and the West End Hotel.

From Sixteenth Street, rows of stately dwellings extend to the Schuylkill, over which a substantial and elegant bridge has recently been thrown. (See BRIDGES.)

BUILDING OF THE MUTUAL LIFE INSURANCE COMPANY OF NEW YORK.

STREETS.—MARKET STREET.

Market Street, from river to river, is the grand *entrepôt* of inland and foreign commerce. Its magnificent width affords ample room and great facilities for the moving of heavy goods; railway tracks are laid down in it, running directly into numerous depots and warehouses, and whole cargoes of merchandise are thus daily sent from the warehouse direct to distant points.

A walk along this street shows many fine buildings, but few of special note. Some are found of historic interest, such as the Old London Coffee-House, on the corner of Front and Market, Penn's House, in Letitia Street, and Christ Church, in Second Street, above Market.

Second Street presents in itself a peculiar feature of the city, which the visitor should not fail to see. It is to Philadelphia what the Bowery is to New York. Of great length, and running in an almost undeviatingly straight line from the northern to the southern portions of the city, it is lined with miles of retail stores of the humbler class, placed with a most supreme disregard for the fitness of things. Hardware, clothing, grocery, confectionery, dry-goods, and almost every other conceivable species of store, follow each other with as little regularity as the scenes in a kaleidoscope.

But, interesting though Second Street is, we cannot linger long here, but must return to the busy, bustling scenes of Market Street. Of the many large business houses on this street, we make special mention of the establishments of Garden & Co., extensive dealers in hats, whose tall, white building is a conspicuous object on Market above Sixth, and that of J. B. Lippincott & Co., one of the largest publishing houses in the world. This establishment is older than the present century, and has risen with the city, from a small beginning to its present mammoth proportions. A good hotel, at a moderate price, will be found in the Bingham House, on the corner of Eleventh and Market (see HOTELS). The square of ground opposite the Bingham House, and bounded by Chestnut, Market, Eleventh, and Twelfth, is one of the monuments of Philadelphia's most munificent benefactor, Stephen Girard. This gentleman left the whole of his enormous wealth to the city of Philadelphia, excepting some minor bequests, amounting, in the aggregate, to between three and four hundred thousand dollars.

The best known of the trusts established by Mr. Girard's will is the celebrated GIRARD COLLEGE (q. v.). Another was the square of ground above described, which is now covered with buildings, and thus tends by its rentals to reduce materially the city taxes.

Immediately opposite a portion of the Girard Square, on the northeast corner of Twelfth and Market, is a huge building known as the "Farmers' Market," and at Broad Street is the new CITY HALL (q. v.), now in course of construction. Two other market-houses, similarly constructed, are situated farther west on this street. Extensive gasworks are situated at Twenty-third and Market.

The Market Street Bridge, a temporary structure, does good service in transporting goods and passengers to the western division of the city. Much of the merchandise and many of the passengers for the Pennsylvania Railroad and its numerous branches cross this bridge; having

J. B. LIPPINCOTT & CO.'S PUBLISHING HOUSE.

done which, they speedily arrive at the Company's two depots, occupying the square on the north side of Market, between Thirty-first and Thirty-second.

Market Street is fast pushing its way westward. Already its line of horse-cars runs to Forty-first Street and thence to the Centennial Exhibition, while a branch extends to Haddington, on the western verge of the city.

This line of cars runs to the celebrated "Kirkbride" Lunatic Asylum, more properly known as the Pennsylvania Hospital for the Insane, the oldest institution of the kind in America. (See HOSPITALS AND ASYLUMS.)

Walnut Street, the chosen haunt of the coal trade, and, to a great extent, of the insurance business, presents many points of interest.

The anthracite coal trade of the Lehigh and Schuylkill regions, which is so important a feature of the domestic industry of Pennsylvania, centres in the lower part of this street, a large four-story building of brown stone, on the corner of Second and Walnut, being entirely given up to this business, and filled with the offices of coal firms. It is known as "Anthracite Block."

A little below Third Street, Walnut Street is crossed diagonally by Dock, and in the triangular space bounded by Third, Dock, and Walnut stands the magnificent building of the Merchants' Exchange. It is an imposing edifice, built of Pennsylvania marble, and, from its conspicuous position, forms the most prominent feature of this part of the city. The spacious rotunda on its eastern side has recently been fitted up in a sumptuous manner for the use of the Board of Brokers.

From the corner of Third Street we pass an almost unbroken file of coal offices, until we reach Fourth Street, and here we turn the corner into Fourth to visit the splendid new offices of the Pennsylvania and the Philadelphia and Reading Railroad Companies, which stand side by side on the east side of Fourth Street, below Walnut.

The office of the Pennsylvania Railroad was built in 1871-2. It is of brick, with an elegant front of Quincy granite, and of dimensions adapted to the business of a corporation which owns and controls more miles of rail than any other in the world. The immense extent of this Company's operations is too well known to need repetition here.

The office of the Reading Railroad was so much enlarged and improved during the summer and fall of 1871 as to make it, in effect, a new building. This, the second road in importance in the State, taps the rich deposits of anthracite coal in the Southern and Middle Coalfields, and carries to market an average of five million tons annually. In 1870 it absorbed the Germantown and Norristown Railroads, and now conducts an enormous passenger traffic over both.

Continuing up Walnut Street, we pass on the left of what was once the "State-House Yard," but has since been named "Independence Square." (See PUBLIC SQUARES.) It is of small dimensions, but the trees are lofty and green overhead, while the ground beneath them has been beaten hard by the tread of countless feet crossing it in every direction.

Diagonally opposite Independence Square is WASHINGTON SQUARE

READING RAILROAD COMPANY'S BUILDING.

(q. v.). Outside the railing of this Square, on the line with Seventh Street, is a stone fountain surmounted by an eagle standing on a globe, which is noteworthy as being the first of those benevolent structures in providing which the Philadelphia Fountain Society has already earned the gratitude of thousands of thirsty men and suffering beasts.

This Society was formed in February, 1869, and erected its first fountain in the succeeding April. From that time to the close of 1874, seventy-three fountains were erected through its efforts, many of them being the gifts of individuals or of societies other than that having the work in special charge, but all given at its instance and through its influence.

What might be termed another benevolent institution, though it is so according to the sound commercial rule of benefiting *both* parties, is the Philadelphia Savings Fund Society (see BANKS AND SAVINGS INSTITUTIONS), whose building stands on the corner of Walnut Street and West Washington Square. This Society, the first of its kind in the country, was established in 1816, and has ever since been eminently successful. All its earnings are appropriated for the benefit of the depositors, with the exception of the amount necessary to meet the working expenses. From a small beginning, the business of the institution has gradually increased, until now its depositors number thirty-nine thousand, and their united deposits exceed ten million dollars.

Trade has not yet pushed its way much on Walnut Street beyond Tenth. From here long rows of substantially-built houses, whose very exteriors have an air of comfort about them, as if they would hint at the ease and plenty within, stretch away almost to the Schuylkill.

The vicinity of Broad and Walnut Streets presents an especially attractive appearance. On the northeast corner is the Dundas Mansion, once celebrated for the exceptional beauty of its grounds ; on the southwest corner the new St. George Hotel presents an imposing appearance, while in the immediate neighborhood are seen the Union League House, the Academy of Music, the Colosseum, etc.

At Eighteenth and Walnut Streets is Rittenhouse Square, one of the finest of the public parks. It is adorned with elaborate drinking-fountains, the gifts of wealthy philanthropists, and is surrounded by elegant and costly dwellings, this being one of the most aristocratic quarters of Philadelphia. An especially noticeable residence is that of Joseph Harrison, Jr., on the east side of the Square, a view of which is herewith presented.

Farther on, at Nineteenth Street, we pass the Church of the Holy Trinity ; at Twenty-first Street the Second Presbyterian Church, a new and elegant structure, and at Twenty-second Street St. James' Church (Episcopal).

UNION LEAGUE

THE **Union League** is a well-known social organization, the outgrowth of a union club which was formed in 1862, for promoting friendly intercourse among loyal people. The organization of the League was effected the same year, and it at once took an active part in all public measures. For several years it wielded a powerful political influence.

UNIVERSITY OF PENNSYLVANIA.

In May, 1865, the present League building (located on Broad Street, above Walnut) was finished, at a cost, including furniture, of about two hundred thousand dollars. It is of brick, in the French Renaissance style, with façades of granite, brick, and brown stone. It has all

UNION LEAGUE.

the appointments of a first-class club-house, and as such has many patrons, the list of members at the present time numbering nearly two thousand.

UNIVERSITY OF PENNSYLVANIA.

The new and elegant buildings of the University of Pennsylvania are located on a square of ground at Thirty-fourth and Locust Streets.

This institution was chartered as a charity school and academy in 1750, and was erected into a college in 1755, and into a university in 1779. It was first located on Fourth Street, below Arch, but was removed to Ninth Street in 1798, and until 1872 occupied two large buildings which stood on the site of the new Post-Office. The old buildings having become inadequate to its wants, the present magnificent structures of serpentine marble were erected, and occupied in 1872. They form one of the handsomest groups of college buildings in the United States.

UNIVERSITY OF PENNSYLVANIA.—DEPARTMENTS OF ARTS AND SCIENCE.

The University is divided into academical, collegiate, medical, and law departments, and among its faculty are numbered some of the most distinguished men in the State.

The junction of Thirty-sixth Street, Darby Road, and Locust Street was selected as the best location for the new buildings of the University. The trustees have erected for the accommodation of the Department of Arts and of Science one of the largest and most conveniently arranged college buildings in the country. This building stands in a square of ground containing more than six acres, and is about two hundred and sixty feet front, by more than one hundred in depth.

WISSAHICKON CREEK

The far-famed Wissahickon, an affluent of the Schuylkill River, is a lovely stream winding through a narrow valley between steep and lofty hills which are wooded to their summits, and have the appearance of a

UP THE WISSAHICKON.

mountain-gorge hundreds of miles from civilization, rather than a pleasure-retreat within the limits of a great city.

In its lower reaches the stream is calm and peaceful, and boats are kept at the two or three small hostelries which stand on its banks, for

WISSAHICKON CREEK.

the convenience of those who wish to row on the placid waters. This calm beauty changes as the valley ascends, and we soon find the stream a mountain torrent, well in keeping with its picturesque situation and surroundings. So with alternate rush of torrent and placid beauty of calm reaches the romantic stream flows down from the high table-lands of Chestnut Hill to its embouchure in the valley of the Schuylkill.

A few manufacturing establishments have invaded the sequestered valley; but the Park Commissioners have taken measures to do away with them all after a certain number of years, and restore the Wissahickon as nearly as possible to its pristine wildness and unfettered beauty.

HERMIT'S POOL.

We may briefly notice a few of the many points of interest in this romantic glen, some of which our artists have sketched in a manner which renders pen-and-ink descriptions superfluous.

Soon after leaving the Schuylkill, the drive up the Wissahickon passes the "Maple Spring" Restaurant, where a curious collection of laurel-roots deftly shaped into all manner of strange or familiar objects, the work of the proprietor, will repay a visit.

A little above this, a lane descends through the woods to the Hermit's

GLEN FERN.

Well, which is said to have been dug by John Kelpius, a German Pietist, who settled down here, with forty followers, two hundred years ago, and lived a hermit's life, waiting for the fulfillment of his dreams. He and his associates gave names to many of the scenes about here, among them the Hermit's Pool, of which we give an illustration.

WISSAHICKON CREEK.

Three and a half miles above its mouth, the stream is crossed by a beautiful structure called the Pipe Bridge, six hundred and eighty-four feet long and one hundred feet above the creek. The water-pipes that supply Germantown with water form the chords of the bridge, the whole being bound together with wrought-iron. It was designed by Frederick Graff, and constructed under his superintendence. A hundred yards above this is the wooden bridge shown in our engraving. Near this is the Devil's Pool, a basin in Creshein Creek, a small tributary of the Wissahickon.

BRIDGE AT VALLEY GREEN.

The next point of interest is the stone bridge at Valley Green, and half a mile beyond this is the first public drinking-fountain e ected in Philadelphia. It was placed here in 1854, and was the precursor of a numerous and beneficial following.

A mile and a half of rugged scenery ensues, terminating in the open sunlight and beautiful landscapes of Chestnut Hill, where the end of the Park is reached.

Watson, in his "Annals of Philadelphia," speaks thus of "The Wissahickon:"

"This romantic creek and scenery, now so much visited and familiar to many, was not long since an extremely wild, unvisited place, to illustrate which I give these facts, to wit: Enoch and Jacob Rittenhouse,

UP THE WISSAHICKON—THE DRIVE.

residents there, told me in 1845 that when they were boys the place had many pheasants; that they snared a hundred of them in a season; they also got many partridges. The creek had many excellent fish, such as large sunfish and perch. The summer wild ducks came there regularly, and were shot often; also, some winter ducks. They then had no visitors from the city, and only occasionally from Germantown. There they lived quietly and retired; now all is public and bustling,—all is changed!".

ZOOLOGICAL GARDEN.

THE **Zoological Garden**, one of the most attractive resorts within the environs of Philadelphia, is situated on the west side of the Schuyl

MONKEY-HOUSE—ZOOLOGICAL GARDEN.

kill River, near its bank, south of Girard Avenue, within the limits of Fairmount Park, and occupies a tract formerly known as "Solitude,"

THE ELEPHANT HOUSE.

THE AVIARY.

and once owned by a grandson of William Penn. This tract, containing thirty-three acres, has been leased by the Park Commissioners to the Zoological Society of Philadelphia, which has fitted it up in a manner best suited for the maintenance and exhibition of birds and animals. The Society intends establishing here a Zoological Garden second to none in the world, and is rapidly carrying out its designs. It has agents in every part of the globe, from whom it receives frequent shipments of rare and interesting specimens of natural history, and is fast filling its ground with specimens of every class of the animal kingdom. Every part of the garden is interesting, but we may mention as the principal features the large and well-filled Carnivora and Monkey-Houses, the Bear Pits, the Aviary, and the Deer Park. All of these

THE BEAR-PITS—ZOOLOGICAL GARDEN.

are already well stocked, and are constantly receiving fresh accessions. The Garden was first opened to the public in July, 1874, and has already become one of the most popular features of the Park. The price of admission is 25 cents for adults, and 10 cents for children.

Visitors reach the Garden by the cars of the Girard Avenue line, which run near the entrance, and with which the various lines running north and south connect by *exchange tickets;* price, nine cents. The steamers on the Schuylkill River also land passengers near the entrance to the Garden.

CARNIVORA BUILDING.

INDEX.

A.

Academy of Fine Arts, 5, 98.
Academy of Music, 8, 98, 108.
Academy of Natural Sciences, 5.
Alexander Presbyterian Church, 45.
Alhambra (Kiralfys'), 12, 98
Almshouse, Blockley, 17, 95.
Amateur Drawing-room, 8.
American Hotel, 67.
American Philosophical Society, 100.
American Sunday-School Union, 6.
American Theatre, Fox's, 10.
Amusements and Audience Halls, 8.
Appraiser's Stores, 99.
Apprentices' Library, 73.
Arch Street, 96.
Arch Street Methodist Church, 44, 98.
Arch Street Opera-House, 8.
Arch Street Presbyterian Church, 46.
Arch Street Theatre, 8, 97.
Assembly Buildings, 8.
Asylums, 62.
Athenæum Library, 73.

B.

Bailey & Co.'s Store, 102.
Baldwin Locomotive Works, 98.
Baltimore Depot, 87, 97.
Bank of America, 13.
Bank of North America, 13, 100.
Banks and Savings Institutions, 13.
Baptist Board of Publication, 102.
Baptist Churches, 42.
Belmont, 17.
Belmont Park, 17.
Beneficial Saving Fund, 14.
Berean Church, 42.
Bethany Church, 45.
Beth-Eden Church, 42, 97.
Bingham House, 68, 104.
Blind Asylum, 62.

Blockley Almsnouse, 17, 95.
Boat Clubs, 17.
Boys' High School, 98.
Bridges, 18.
Broad Street, 97.
Bulletin, Evening, 100.
Burd Orphan Asylum, 63.

C.

Calvary Church, 46.
Camden and Atlantic R. R. Depot, 89.
Cape May Railroad Depot, 91.
Carncross & Dixey's Minstrels, 10.
Carpenter's Hall, 24.
Cathedral, 48.
Cathedral Cemetery, 26.
Cemeteries, 26.
Centennial Exhibition, 29.
Centennial National Bank, 14.
Central Congregational Church, 43.
Central High School, 98.
Central National Bank, 14.
Chamber of Commerce, 99.
Chambers Presbyterian Church, 46.
Chamouni, 61.
Chestnut Street, 99.
Chestnut Street Bridge, 18.
Chestnut Street Theatre, 8, 102.
Christ Church (Episcopal), 46, 104.
Christ Church (German Reformed), 48
Christ Church Hospital, 63.
Churches, 41.
Church of the Assumption, 48.
Church of the Messiah, 50.
Church of the Restoration, 50.
City Hall, 50, 104.
City National Bank, 14.
College of Pharmacy, 77.
College of Physicians, 75.
Colonnade Hotel, 68, 102.
Colosseum, 10, 98.
Columbia Bridge, 18.

Commercial National Bank, 14.
Commonwealth National Bank, 14.
Concert Hall, 10, 102.
Concordia Hall, 10.
Congregational Churches, 43.
Connecting Railroad Bridge, 20, 58.
Consolidation National Bank, 14.
Continental Hotel, 68, 102.
Corn Exchange National Bank, 14.
Custom House, 52, 100.

D.

Deaf and Dumb Asylum, 63, 97.
Delaware River, 52.
Dental Colleges, 77.
Depots (Railroad), 87.
Drexel & Co., 100.
Dundas Mansion, 108.

E.

Eastern Penitentiary, 83.
Egglesfield Entrance, 59.
Eighth National Bank, 14.
Eleventh Street Opera-House, 10.
Epiphany Church, 47.
Episcopal Churches, 46.
Episcopal Hospital, 63.
Evening Bulletin, 100.
Evening Telegraph, 100.

F.

Fairmount Bridge, 20.
Fairmount Park, 55.
Falls of Schuylkill Bridge, 22.
Falls Railroad Bridge, 22.
Falls Village, 95.
Farmers' and Mechanics' National Bank, 14, 100.
Farmers' Market, 104.
Fidelity Insurance Company, 91, 100.
Fifth Baptist Church, 42.
Fifth Presbyterian Church, 46.
Fine Arts, Academy of, 5.
First Baptist Church, 43.
First City Troop, 79.
First Moravian Church, 45.
First National Bank, 14.
First Presbyterian Church, 46.
First Reformed Church (Dutch), 48.
First Reformed Church (German), 48.
First Unitarian Church, 50.
First Universalist Church, 50.
Forrest Mansion Garden, 10.
Fourth Baptist Church, 43.
Fox's American Theatre, 10.
Frankford Arsenal, 79.
Franklin Institute, 61.
Franklin's Grave, 96, 97.

Franklin Square, 83.
Friends' Asylum for the Insane, 65.
Friends' Meetings, 44.

G.

Garden & Co.'s Store, 104.
Gas Works, 95.
George's Hill, 29, 61.
German Hospital, 65.
Girard Avenue Bridge, 22, 57, 95.
Girard College, 61.
Girard House, 68, 102.
Girard Life Annuity and Trust Company, 91.
Girard National Bank, 14.
Girard Point Elevator, 95.
Glenwood Cemetery, 27.
Gloria Dei Church, 47.
Grace Church (Methodist), 45.
Graff's Monument, 56, 57.
Grand Central Variety Theatre, 10.
Grant's Cottage, 57.
Gray Reserves, 79.
Gray's Ferry Bridge, 22.
Guarantee Trust and Safe Deposit Company, 91, 100.
Guy's Hotel, 68.

H.

Hahnemann Medical College, 77.
Handel and Haydn Hall, 12.
Hebrew Churches, 44.
High School for Boys, 98.
Holy Communion Church, 44.
Holy Trinity Church, 47, 108.
Horticultural Hall, 12, 98.
Hospitals and Asylums, 62.
Hospital of the Protestant Episcopal Church, 63.
Hospital of the University of Pennsylvania, 65.
Hotel Lafayette, 98.
Hotels, 67.
House of Refuge, 83.

I.

Incarnation, Church of, 99.
Independence Hall, 71.
Independence Square, 85.
Inquirer, 100.

J.

Jefferson Medical College, 77.

K.

Keystone Bank, 14.
Keystone Battery, 79.

INDEX.

Kiralfys' Alhambra, 12.
Kirkbride's Lunatic Asylum, 106.

L.

Lansdowne, 59.
La Pierre House, 70, 98.
Laurel Hill Cemetery, 27, 95.
League Island Navy Yard, 73, 93, 97.
Ledger Building, 100.
Lemon Hill, 56, 95.
Libraries, 73.
Lincoln Monument, 56, 58.
Lippincott & Co. (J. B.), 104.
Logan Square, 85.
London Coffee House, 104.
Lutheran Churches, 44.

M.

Manufacturers' National Bank, 14.
Marine Hospital, 95.
Market Street, 104.
Market Street Bridge, 24, 104.
Masonic Temple, 75, 98, 102.
Mechanics' Cemetery, 27.
Mechanics' National Bank, 14.
Medical Schools, 75.
Memorial Baptist Church, 43
Mercantile Library, 73.
Merchants' Exchange, 106.
Merchants' Hotel, 70.
Methodist Book Rooms, 97.
Methodist Episcopal Churches, 44.
Mikve Israel, 44.
Military Establishments, 79.
Mint, 80, 102.
Monument Cemetery, 27.
Moravian Church (First), 45.
Mount Moriah Cemetery, 27.
Mount Peace Cemetery, 27.
Mount Pleasant, 95.
Mount Vernon Cemetery, 27.
Moyamensing Prison, 83.
Musical Fund Hall, 12.
Mutual Life Insurance Company of New York, 102.

N.

National Bank of Commerce, 14.
National Bank of the Northern Liberties, 14.
National Bank of the Republic, 14.
National Guards, 79.
National Security Bank, 14.
Natural Sciences, Academy of, 5.
Naval Asylum, 65.
New Church (Swedenborgian), 45.
New National Theatre, 12.
North Broad Street Church, 46.

Northern Savings Fund Society, 14, 91.
North Pennsylvania Railroad Depot, 89.

O.

Odd Fellows' Cemetery, 27.
Old London Coffee House, 104.
Old Swedes Church, 47.

P.

Penn National Bank, 14.
Penn's House, 104.
Pennsylvania Asylum for the Deaf and Dumb, 63.
Pennsylvania Company for Insurances on Lives, etc., 91, 100.
Pennsylvania Hospital, 65.
Pennsylvania Hospital for the Insane, 67.
Pennsylvania Institution for the Blind, 62.
Pennsylvania Railroad Depots, 89.
Pennsylvania Railroad Offices, 106.
Penn Treaty Monument, 81.
Penn Trust and Safe Deposit Co., 91.
People's Bank, 14.
People's National Bank, 14.
Peters' Island, 95.
Pharmacy, College of, 77.
Philadelphia Bank, 100.
Philadelphia College of Pharmacy, 77.
Philadelphia Hospital, 67.
Philadelphia Inquirer, 100.
Philadelphia Library, 75.
Philadelphia National Bank, 15.
Philadelphia Savings Fund, 15, 108.
Philosophical Society, 100.
Philadelphia Trust, Safe Deposit, and Insurance Company, 91.
Point Breeze Gas Works, 95.
Post-Office, 52, 81, 100, 102.
Presbyterian Board of Publication, 102.
Presbyterian Churches, 45.
Prisons, 83.
Protestant Episcopal Churches, 46.
Provident Life and Trust Company, 91.
Public Buildings, 50, 104.
Public Squares, 83.

R.

Railroad Depots, 87.
Reading Railroad Depot, 89, 98.
Reading Railroad Offices, 106.
Red Star Line of Steamers, 95.
Reform Club, 102.
Reformed Churches, 48.
Ridgway Library, 75, 97.
Rittenhouse Square, 87, 108.
Rockland Mansion, 95.
Rodef Sholem, 44, 98.
Roman Catholic Churches, 48.

S.

Safe Deposit Companies, 91.
Saint Andrew's Church, 47.
Saint Augustine's Church, 48.
Saint Clement's Church, 47.
Saint Cloud Hotel, 70, 97.
Saint Elmo Hotel, 70.
Saint George Hotel, 70, 98, 108.
Saint George's Church, 45.
Saint James's Church, 47.
Saint John's Church, 48.
Saint John's (Lutheran) Church, 44.
Saint Joseph's Church, 48.
Saint Joseph's Hospital, 67.
Saint Mark's (Episcopal) Church, 47.
Saint Mark's (Lutheran) Church, 44.
Saint Mary's Church, 48.
Saint Paul's Church, 47.
Saint Peter's Church (Catholic), 50.
Saint Peter's Church (Episcopal), 47.
Saint Stephen's Church, 47.
Saint Stephen's Hotel, 70.
School of Design, 98.
Schuylkill Arsenal, 79.
Schuylkill River, 93.
Schuylkill Water-Works, 56.
Second Presbyterian Church, 46.
Second Reformed Church (Dutch), 48.
Sedgely Park, 57.
Seventh National Bank, 15.
Simmons & Slocum's Minstrels, 8, 97.
Sixth National Bank, 15.
Society of Friends, 44.
Solitude, 58, 117.
South Street Bridge, 24.
Southwark National Bank, 15.
Spring Garden Bank, 15.
Spring Garden Street Church, 45.
Strawberry Mansion, 95.
Streets, 96.
Sunday-school Union, 6.
Swedenborgian Church, 45.
Swedes Church (Gloria Dei), 47.
Sweet Brier Mansion, 59.

T.

Tabernacle Baptist Church, 43.
Tabernacle Presbyterian Church, 46.
Third National Bank, 15.
Times Office, 102.
Tom Moore's Cottage, 95.

Tradesmen's National Bank, 15.
Trinity Methodist Church, 45.

U.

Union Banking Company, 15.
Union League, 98, 108.
Union National Bank, 15.
Unitarian Church, 50.
United States Appraiser's Stores, 99.
United States Arsenal, 95.
United States Banking Company, 15.
United States Marine Hospital, 95.
United States Mint, 102.
United States Naval Asylum, 65.
Universalist Churches, 50.
University Hospital, 65.
University of Pennsylvania, 110.
University of Pennsylvania, Medical Department, 79.

W.

Walnut Street, 106.
Walnut Street Theatre, 13.
Washington Grays, 80.
Washington Hotel, 71.
Washington Square, 87, 106.
West Arch Street Church, 46.
West Chester Depot, 91.
West End Hotel, 71, 102.
Western National Bank, 17.
Western Saving Fund Society, 17.
West Jersey Railroad Depot, 91.
West Laurel Hill Cemetery, 27.
West Philadelphia Bank, 17.
Wills Hospital, 67.
Wissahickon Bridges, 24.
Wissahickon Creek, 112.
Women's Medical College, 79.
Woodland Cemetery, 29.
Wood's Museum, 13.

Y.

Young Men's Christian Association, 102.

Z.

Zion (Lutheran) Church, 44.
Zoological Garden, 95, 118.

BLOOMSDALE.

Great, and varied to an extent almost unexampled elsewhere, are the natural resources and industrial interests of Pennsylvania.

In mineral and other deposits none can compare with her; in the mechanism and skill which converts her ores from their crude condition into the ponderous, delicate, or minute forms useful to man, her sons are not excelled within or without the Union.

The ingenuity of Pennsylvania artisans is, in every branch of industry, almost world-wide; her locomotives traverse every road in Europe, and her iron ships, afloat and being built (a comparatively new outlet for her enterprise, making the Delaware the rival of the Clyde), are destined to spread her fame wherever American commerce reaches. In view of such well-earned reputation, with such mechanical and artistic record, how fitting it is her *tillage*, on which commerce, manufactures, and industry of every kind repose, should be esteemed noteworthy. It is pleasant to know that her fertile soil, her intelligent husbandmen, her crops, and flocks, and herds may be referred to as justly entitled to high discriminating praise. It is true we have not within our borders broad prairies like unto those of the far West, nor its unctuous soil which knows no depth, and ever yields without exhaustion of fertility. We glory in the natural wealth of our sister States—their prosperity is ours as well; but in our mines of coal, and iron, and other minerals, in our ceaseless flow of oil, nature has dealt kindly by us also. The gold of California, the cotton of the South, the sugar of Louisiana and Texas, the silks and other fibres of the world, the spices and coffees of the tropics, the highest mechanism of Europe, its best efforts in the useful and fine arts, are all at our command; we have only to stretch forth our hands and grasp what has been so bountifully placed within our reach; what has been denied us in nature's profuse scattering we have gained by thoughtful, well-directed efforts in the rotation of crops, in the application of appropriate fertilizers, and other means intelligently directed to a desired end, until "Pennsylvania Agriculture" has become simply another term for high-farming and successful tillage, whilst those who, resident at distant points, seek the best; whether it be the fine strains of animals which graze its rich pastures, or the seeds of grasses, cereals, or vegetables, bend their steps hitherward, and never go empty away.

On the Delaware, a few miles above Philadelphia, and adjoining that fertile tract known as Penn's Manor, a wise and discriminating reservation of the proprietary Governor is BLOOMSDALE, which we have selected as illustrative of the rural industry of Pennsylvania. This estate, we do not hesitate to say, has contributed, in an especially large degree, to the public good, by its products and by its eminent example also. Bloomsdale may be assumed a model of intelligent industry, systematic culture, and rural progress. It embraces within its boundaries, independent of outlying lands, five hundred acres devoted to the culture and product of *seeds*, known in every hamlet, almost on every farm-hold and country homestead, as "Landreth's,"—known almost equally well on the banks of the Missouri, the Mississippi, and the Ganges,—for it should be stated, to the business credit and reputation of the firm, that for three generations Landreth's Seeds have been annually shipped to India, and are preferred by Englishmen resident in Hindostan to the seeds of their own native land, our climate ripening them better than the humid air of England.

It is the modest motto of the proprietors of Bloomsdale that "Landreth's Seeds speak their own praise." They certainly cannot have done so with feeble voice, for not only are those broad acres taxed to their utmost productive power, but nearly approaching one thousand other acres in addition, owned, occupied, and cultivated by the firm, are devoted to seed culture; by this it is not intended to designate lands simply tributary, tilled by their owners who raise crops on contract, without direct control of those who have bargained for the product (as it is the custom with seed-merchants thus to obtain supplies), but immediate, active personal care and supervision. Thus an idea may be conceived, though necessarily imperfect, of the activity of mind and energy called forth by such extended operations; but system and order are ever triumphant, and in the case in point the adage is aptly illustrated. With increased acreage has come increased reputation, and Pennsylvania may claim the credit, not a slight one we opine, of having conducted within her borders a seed trade larger than exists elsewhere (if lands be taken as the measure), not alone within the Union, but without as well. Europe, travelers assert, can exhibit nothing of like extent. This is no idle boast, made in the interest of private enterprise or pride of commonwealth.

Independent of the numerous workmen employed on the estate,—many of whom have been life-long *attaches* of the establishment, occupying cottages on the premises, and as much at home as the proprietors themselves—a pleasing feature which it were well to imitate,—there are three steam-engines for threshing, winnowing and cleaning seeds, grinding feed, etc.; a "caloric" for pumping; and an admirably well-adjusted steaming apparatus for preparing food for the working stock. But it may be still more worthy of note, that for a term protracted through several years, energetic experiments in ploughing by steam have been conducted by the Messrs. Landreth, at Bloomsdale, using the direct-traction engine of Williamson, with Thomson's India-rubber tire. At first, and for months, great hope of success was entertained; but unforeseen difficulties in the way of direct traction exhibited themselves. At present, the purpose is to adopt the "Rope System," as successfully practiced in England, using the Williamson engine as the moving power. It is simply right to chronicle their efforts in this direction in a volume descriptive of our State, the record, as it were, of its status at the present day. As the early efforts in river and ocean navigation are referred to with ever-increasing interest as progress is made in that direction, so will in the future be those of *tillage by steam*, and our State is entitled to its due share of praise with respect to land, as it unquestionably is to Fitch's exertions in steam navigation.

Limited space prohibits many of the details of the operations at Bloomsdale, which we would gladly give our readers; the sketch annexed may, however, convey some idea of the extent of the structures required for the storage, drying, and preservation of crops, and otherwise successful prosecution of the peculiar business there conducted, which is a credit to the proprietors, the successors of those who founded the business in 1784, and which may be classed as prominent among the many industrial enterprises of Pennsylvania.

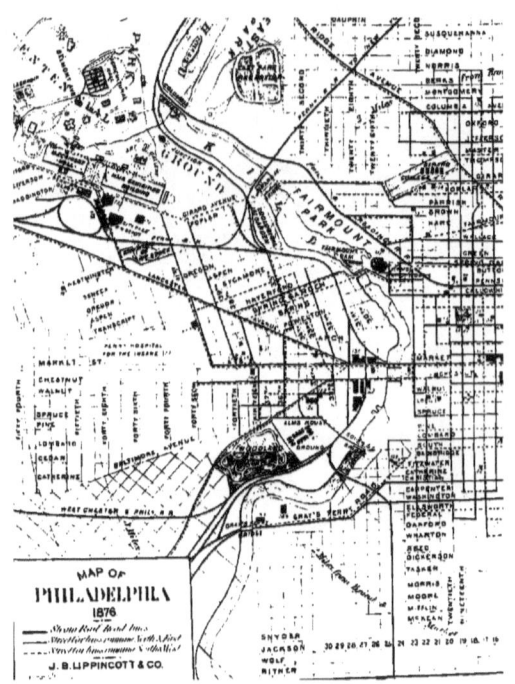

THE QUALITY OF THE
"STAR" ALPACA BRAIDS

HAS BEEN FAIRLY TESTED BY THE LADIES THROUGHOUT THE COUNTRY, AND THE POPULARITY THEY HAVE GAINED IN COMPETITION WITH OTHER MAKES IS EVIDENCE ENOUGH OF THEIR SUPERIORITY.

Letters of Recommendation from 1000 Dressmakers in Philadelphia and Baltimore.

HIGHEST AWARD (SILVER MEDAL), FRANKLIN INSTITUTE EXHIBITION, 1874.
HIGHEST AWARD (SILVER MEDAL), MARYLAND INSTITUTE EXHIBITION, 1874.
HIGHEST AWARD (SILVER MEDAL), CINCINNATI INDUST'L EXHIBITION, 1875.

KILBURN & GATES,

WHOLESALE MANUFACTURERS OF

COTTAGE FURNITURE,

619 Market St., and 608, 610, 612, 613, 615, & 617 Commerce St.,

PHILADELPHIA, PA.

AN EXTENSIVE ASSORTMENT OF

ORNAMENTED CHAMBER SUITES.

Also, a great variety of *Bureaus, Washstands, Wardrobes, Bedsteads,* and all other goods peculiar to this branch of trade, in plain finish, at reasonable prices. Every article warranted. Dealers are respectfully invited to call or send for Catalogue.

The largest establishment in the United States devoted exclusively to the production of

COTTAGE FURNITURE.

GOLD PENS,

Pen and Pencil Cases, Pencils and Holders,

MANUFACTURED BY

MABIE, TODD & CO., NEW YORK,

ARE

For Sale by the leading Stationers and Jewelers

IN THE UNITED STATES.

A full line of our goods displayed in Main Building, Centennial Exhibition.

TRUST AND SAFE DEPOSIT COMPANY.

The Pennsylvania Company for Insurances on Lives

AND GRANTING ANNUITIES,

431 CHESTNUT STREET.

Incorporated March 10, 1812.   Charter Perpetual.

Capital, $2,000,000. | Surplus, $1,000,000.

Income Collected and Remitted.
Interest allowed on Money Deposits.
Safes in their Burglar-proof Vaults for Rent.

The Protection of their Vaults for the Preservation of Wills offered gratuitously.

GOLD AND SILVER PLATE, DEEDS, MORTGAGES, ETC., RECEIVED FOR SAFE-KEEPING UNDER GUARANTEE.

LINDLEY SMYTH, *President*.   LILBURN H. STEEL, *Treasurer*.
JARVIS MASON, *Trust Officer*.   WILLIAM B. HILL, *Actuary*.

DIRECTORS:

Lindley Smyth,	Charles Dutilh,	William S. Vaux,	Adolph E. Borie,
Alexander Biddle,	Joshua B. Lippincott,	Chas. H. Hutchinson,	George A. Wood,
Anthony J. Antelo,	Charles S. Lewis,	Henry Lewis,	Jacob P. Jones,
	Henry M. Phillips.		

Calvary Songs.

A NEW HYMN AND TUNE BOOK FOR THE FAMILY AND THE SUNDAY SCHOOL.

Prepared by Rev. Chas. S. Robinson, D.D., and Theodore E. Perkins.

Containing many new and old pieces, and nearly all the popular music sung in revival meetings by Mr. Sankey, Mr. Weeks, and Mr. Bliss.

35 Cents per Copy. $30.00 per 100 Copies.

Specimen pages furnished upon application.   Just published and for sale by

The American Sunday-School Union,

1122 Chestnut Street, Philadelphia.—A. Kirkpatrick.

10 Bible House, New York.—G. S. Scofield.   40 Winter Street, Boston.—J. A. Crowley.
98 Dearborn St., Chicago.—W. R. Port.   257 N. Sixth Street, St. Louis.—S. Paxson.

HOOD, BONBRIGHT & CO.,

MARKET ST., PHILADELPHIA,

IMPORTERS AND JOBBERS OF

European and American Dry Goods,

NOTIONS, WHITE GOODS, FURNISHING GOODS, CARPETING, ETC.

Always in Store many Choice Brands of the Celebrated Philadelphia made Goods.
LOWEST PRICES AND BEST INDUCEMENTS GUARANTEED.

THE OLD PENN MUTUAL.

There is in the public mind an under-strata of clear, good sense, touching vital questions in general. While gaudy demonstrations of any kind will always attract a considerable amount of patronage and applause, the fact still remains that the public, as a whole, appreciate that the most which has in it the greatest substantial good. And life insurance is no exception to this rule. Those companies which have the most of evident integrity and enduring worth are those which in the long run secure constantly increasing favor at the hands of the people. To the operation of this rule is manifestly attributable the growing success which attaches to any of the companies which are now before the public, and most overwhelmingly is it true in the case of the Penn Mutual Life Insurance Company.

This Company justly ranks as one of the most reputable in all essential points in the country. It is ripe in years, grandly conservative yet justly liberal in management, and so evidently straightforward and conscientious in its course of action as to be singularly free from the criticisms and taunts which so often appear against insurance companies.

Our attention has been especially drawn to it upon this occasion through the appearance of its *twenty-eighth* annual statement, recently published. The Company increased in assets largely, in the amount of receipts over that of 1874, in the insurance in force, in the number of policies issued over the number of the previous year, and most decidedly in the matter of its net condition. In other words, notwithstanding the dull times of 1875, and the general falling off of the life insurance business, the Penn is not only to-day much richer in net condition, but much richer also in gross condition, than at any previous period of its history. To those familiar with the business it is not necessary to suggest the significance of an exhibit which shows, upon the New York basis of reserve, a surplus over liabilities of nearly twenty per cent. of the gross assets. Yet this is what the Penn Mutual shows, its assets being on January 1st, $5,504,329.24, and its liabilities on a four and a half per cent. reserve, $4,421,238.00, leaving a surplus of $1,083,091.24. On a four per cent. basis the liabilities are $4,756,438.00 and the surplus $747,891.24,—nearly fifteen per cent. of the gross assets. This showing is of course equally remarkable with the other, and reflects the highest honor upon the Company. The assets were increased during 1873, $913,565.69, and its surplus (New York standard) some $350,000. Its total income was about $400,000 larger than during the previous year, and its total expenditures were only $158,529 greater. On the other hand, the dividends paid to policy-holders during 1875 were several thousands of dollars greater than in 1874.

HALE, KILBURN & CO.,

48 and 50 North Sixth Street, Philadelphia,

AND

613 Broadway, New York,

SOLE MANUFACTURERS OF THE

"Champion" Folding Bedstead and Crib,

THE "EVERITT" BEDSTEAD.

SUPERIOR TO ANY OTHER.

UNCHALLENGED! UNEQUALLED!

HALE'S FLEXIBLE TOP SPRING BED.

Hale's Flexible Seat Chairs, etc.   Hale's Chameleon Mirror Frames.

General Manufacturers of

FINE WALNUT WORK.

Many Styles of Plain and Elaborate

PIER AND MANTEL MIRRORS,

PICTURE FRAMES, MOULDINGS, Etc., Etc.

Office and Salesroom,

48 and 50 North Sixth Street, Philadelphia.

Branch Store,

No. 613 Broadway, New York.

Factories, 48 & 50 N. Sixth St., 615-621 Filbert St., Phila.

ESTABLISHED 1821.

MORRIS, TASKER & CO., Limited,

PASCAL IRON WORKS,
PHILADELPHIA.

DELAWARE IRON COMPANY,
NEW CASTLE, DEL.

OFFICES: { No. 209 South Third Street, Philadelphia.
No. 15 Gold Street, New York.
No. 36 Oliver Street, Boston.

MANUFACTURERS OF

WROUGHT IRON WELDED TUBES,
Plain, Galvanized, and Rubber Coated,
FOR GAS, STEAM, AND WATER.

LAP-WELDED CHARCOAL IRON BOILER TUBES.

Oil Well Tubing and Casing, Gas and Steam Fittings, Brass Valves and Cocks, Gas- and Steam-Fitters' Tools, Cast-Iron Gas and Water Pipe, Street Lamp-Posts and Lanterns, Improved Coal Gas Apparatus, Improved Sugar Machinery, etc.

WE WOULD CALL SPECIAL ATTENTION TO OUR PATENT VULCANIZED RUBBER-COATED TUBE.

To guard against misrepresentations, and insure buyers of **Tube and Boiler Tube** their obtaining the standard article, we stamp each length of our manufacture with Registered Trade Mark, and would call especial attention to our weights, as we still **adhere to thickness adopted by us forty years ago.**

ESTABLISHED 1818.

WILLIAM STRUTHERS.   JOHN STRUTHERS.   WILLIAM STRUTHERS, Jr.

STRUTHERS & SONS,

Marble, Granite, and Sandstone Works

IMPORTERS OF SCOTCH GRANITE AND ALL FOREIGN MARBLES.

Designs furnished for Monumental Work, Mantels & all inside Decoration.

A large assortment of New Mantels of the Latest Design constantly on hand.

CARVING A SPECIALTY.

Contractors for the Marble Work of the New Public Buildings.

Office, Studio, and Warerooms, 1022 Market Street,

Steam Works, Walnut Street Wharf, Schuylkill,

PHILADELPHIA.

THE KEYSTONE BRIDGE COMPANY,

BUILDERS OF

LONG SPAN BRIDGES,

Steel, Iron, and Wooden Railway and Road Bridges, Iron Roof-Trusses, Wrought-Iron Turn-Tables, Buildings,

"LINVILLE & PIPER" PATENT WROUGHT-IRON BRIDGES,

"Wrought-Iron Riveted and Rivetless Columns" for Bridges and Buildings, Buckle Plates, Hydraulic Forgings,

AND

"UPSET EYE-BARS,"

PIVOT BRIDGES, IRON VIADUCTS, IRON PIERS, SUSPENSION BRIDGES, COMPOSITE BRIDGES, BRIDGE BOLTS, AND GENERAL MACHINE WORK.

Office and Works, 51st and Harrison Sts. (18th Ward), Pittsburgh, Pa.

Western Office, Cor. Randolph and La Salle Sts., Chicago.

Album of designs and description of important bridges sent free on application to J. H. LINVILLE, President, 128 South Fourth Street, Philadelphia.

The Keystone Bridge Company has able and experienced bridge engineers at its principal offices, who will examine localities and advise as to the best methods and plans for replacing existing bridges, and furnish designs and specifications for new bridges. These examinations will have the special attention of the President and General Managers of the Company, who are practical constructors of great experience.

 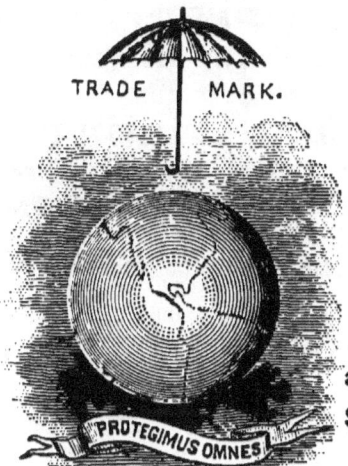

Umbrellas.
SUPERIOR TO ANY OTHER MAKE,

Parasols.
Parasols of our make are always the Leading Styles of the Season.

MANUFACTURED AND FOR SALE BY

WILLIAM A. DROWN & CO.,
246 Market St., Philadelphia. 498 & 500 Broadway, New York.

Our name is on such qualities as we can confidently recommend. Ask the retailers for them.

THE FIDELITY
Insurance, Trust, and Safe Deposit Company.
327-331 CHESTNUT ST., PHILADELPHIA.

Capital - - - - - - $2,000,000.

SECURITIES and VALUABLES taken for SAFE-KEEPING, UNDER GUARANTEE.

SAFES RENTED IN BURGLAR AND FIRE-PROOF VAULTS, KEYS EXCLUSIVELY WITH RENTER.

Deposits of Money taken on Interest.

COLLECTIONS MADE ON COMMISSION. TRUSTS EXECUTED. ES-TATES ADMINISTERED. LETTERS OF CREDIT FURNISHED. WILLS TAKEN FOR SAFE-KEEPING.

STEPHEN A. CALDWELL, Prest.   JOHN B. GEST, Vice-Prest.
ROBERT PATTERSON, Sec'y and Treas.

DIRECTORS:

Stephen A. Caldwell, Clarence H. Clark, John Welsh, Edward W. Clark, Alexander Henry, George F. Tyler, Henry C. Gibson, J. Gillingham Fell, Henry Pratt McKean, William H. Merrick, John B. Gest.

J. B. LIPPINCOTT & CO.,
715 AND 717 MARKET STREET, PHILADELPHIA,

INVITE ATTENTION TO THEIR

Book and Job Printing Department,

IN WHICH THEY ARE PREPARED TO EXECUTE,

WITH TASTE AND PROMPTNESS,

ALL ORDERS FOR

BOOKS, PAMPHLETS, CIRCULARS, BILL HEADS, BLANK FORMS, INVITATIONS, CARDS, ETC.

☞ Estimates and specimens furnished by mail on application.

BREECH-LOADING
FIRE ARMS.
JOS. C. GRUBB & CO.,
No. 712 Market Street, Philadelphia,

DEALERS IN ALL KINDS OF

BREECH- and MUZZLE-LOADING, Single- and Double-Barrel GUNS, RIFLES, and PISTOLS, Ammunition and Appurtenances for the same.

GUN MATERIAL OF ALL KINDS.

J. & P. COATS'S
Best Six-Cord Spool Cotton,

Warranted 200 Yards.

Six-Cord in all numbers from 8 to 100 inclusive.

FOR HAND AND MACHINE, WHITE, BLACK, AND COLORED.

BATES & COATES, Agents,

No. 209 Church Street, Philadelphia.

JAMES W. QUEEN & CO.,
Mathematical, Optical, and Philosophical Instruments,

924 CHESTNUT STREET, PHILADELPHIA.

Drawing Instruments and Drawing Materials,   Spectacles, Spy Glasses,
Opera Glasses, Field Glasses,   Microscopes, Magic Lanterns,
Thermometers. Barometers, Philosophical Apparatus.

The following Catalogues sent by mail, on receipt of *ten cents* for each part:

Part 1st, Mathematical; Part 2d, Optical; Part 3d, Magic Lanterns; Part 4th, Philosophical.

MARCY'S SCIOPTICON

IS A GREATLY IMPROVED FORM OF

MAGIC LANTERN

FOR OIL OR LIME LIGHT.

For Homes, Sunday-Schools, and Lecture-Rooms

IT STANDS UNRIVALED.

It is safe, compact, portable, always ready, easy to use, steady in its action, the only reliable instrument capable of giving satisfactory illumination without resort to chemical lights. With MARCY'S TRIPLE JET, it gives us the three forms of lime light, each at its best, with its cost and difficulties reduced to a minimum.

Circulars, and a choice selected list of "NEW DEPARTURE" Magic-Lantern Slides, will be forwarded on application, free. The Sciopticon Manual, 5th edition, including catalogue, 50 cents. Address,

L. J. MARCY,

1340 Chestnut St., Philadelphia.

(Opposite the United States Mint.)

DREXEL & CO.,

Bankers,

No. 34 SOUTH THIRD STREET, PHILADELPHIA.

DREXEL, MORGAN & CO.,   DREXEL, HARJES & CO.,

Broad and Wall Streets,   *31 Boulevard Haussmann,*

NEW YORK.   **PARIS.**

ISSUE

Commercial and Traveler's Letter of Credit and Bills of Exchange on all parts of Europe. Negotiate State, Municipal, and R. R. Securities.

BUY AND SELL GOVERNMENT BONDS, STOCKS, AND GOLD.

TRANSACT A GENERAL BANKING BUSINESS.

---

128 WILLIAM STREET,   **27 N. SIXTH STREET,**
NEW YORK.   PHILADELPHIA.

JESSUP & MOORE,
PAPER MANUFACTURERS.

IMPORTERS OF

PAPER MAKERS' SUPPLIES.

MAKE TO ORDER, AND HAVE IN STORE,

WRITING PAPER,   **COPPER-PLATE PAPERS,**
Standard Sizes and Weight.   *Standard Sizes and Weight.*

LITHOGRAPH PAPERS,
Standard Sizes and Weight.

SUPER-CALENDERED BOOK,
(VARIOUS TINTS.) Standard Sizes and Weight.

BOOK PAPER,   **NEWSPAPER,**
Standard Sizes and Weight.   *Standard Sizes and Weight.*

☞ Samples sent upon application.

AMERICAN
LIFE INSURANCE COMPANY
OF PHILADELPHIA,

S. E. Corner Fourth and Walnut Streets.

ASSETS - - - - - - - $5,000,000.

HASELTINE'S ART GALLERIES,
Nos. 1125 and 1127 Chestnut Street,
(Second and Upper Floors,)
PHILADELPHIA.

Always on exhibition Free, and for sale, the largest collection of
PAINTINGS AND STATUARY
belonging to any dealer in the UNITED STATES. An immense collection of Braun's Autotypes.

The famous Paintings of JERUSALEM, ANCIENT AND MODERN, being two of the great works of art of the age, on special exhibition apart from other pictures.

All matters pertaining to Art attended to by the Establishment.

ASSETS, OVER THREE MILLIONS.

Provident Life and Trust Company,
OF PHILADELPHIA.
INCORPORATED THIRD MONTH 22, 1865.

PROMINENT FEATURES:

I. Low rate of mortality, consequent upon great care in the selection of lives, and the large proportion of Friends among its members.
II. Economy in expenses.
III. Prudent investment of Money.
IV. Liberality to the insured; as, for example, its NON-FORFEITURE SYSTEM, which is more liberal than that guaranteed by the Massachusetts law.

The mortality experience of the Company for the last eight years has been an average of only three-quarters of one per cent., while the general average of American Companies has been much in excess of that rate. The losses of the Company by death in 1875 have been even less than the above average, the percentage being but one-half of one per cent. These results have been realized only by maintaining a high standard of medical examination in the selection of risks.

Send for Circular. **OFFICE, No. 108 SOUTH FOURTH ST.**

ZOOLOGICAL GARDEN,

FAIRMOUNT PARK, PHILADELPHIA.

This beautiful Garden, laid out with the greatest taste of the Landscape Gardener's Art, replete with Botanical and Floral beauties, and containing the largest collection of Beasts, Birds, and Reptiles in America, is **OPEN EVERY DAY**. Admission, 25 cents for adults, 10 cents for children. Accessible by all City Passenger Railways, and Schuylkill River Steamboats.

A MAGNIFICENT RESTAURANT IS ERECTED IN THE GARDEN,

where all the delicacies of the season, and substantial meals and refreshments, are served by Ferd. Hardt, who will make special contracts with excursionists, or serve by the card at moderate rates.

CHARLES MAGARGE & CO.,

WHOLESALE DEALERS IN

Paper and Paper Makers' Materials.

WAREHOUSE,

30, 32, and 34 SOUTH SIXTH STREET,

PHILADELPHIA, PA.

The undersigned offer to the Trade the following: Map, Plate, and Printing Papers; Blank Book Papers (comprising best makes); Cap, Letter, Note, Blotting Papers, etc.; Bond Papers; Press Boards; Tissues; Manilla.

PAPER MAKERS' MATERIALS.—Imported and Domestic Rags, Bleaching Salts, Wire Cloths, Feltings, Ultramarine.

Papers made to order at short notice, at our Wissahickon and Hanwell Mills.

CHARLES MAGARGE & CO.

LIPPINCOTT'S MAGAZINE.

AN ILLUSTRATED MONTHLY OF

POPULAR LITERATURE AND SCIENCE.

The great object and constant aim of the conductors of LIPPINCOTT'S MAGAZINE are to supply their patrons with literary entertainments of a refined and varied character, as well as to present in a graphic and striking manner the most recent information and the soundest views concerning subjects of general interest. The Publishers would respectfully solicit attention to the following characteristics of the Magazine, all of which combine to render each issue an agreeable and instructive compendium of

POPULAR READING.

SERIAL NOVELS of a highly attractive order by able and brilliant writers, both at home and abroad.

SHORT STORIES distinguished for the charm and diversity of their sentiment, and for the simplicity and elegance of their style.

ESSAYS AND NARRATIVES treating clearly and briefly of important social, literary, historical and political subjects.

SKETCHES OF TRAVEL in various sections of the world, by experienced authors, beautifully and extensively illustrated.

PAPERS ON SCIENCE AND ART, recording in a popular manner the most notable discoveries and most striking productions in these departments of culture.

LITERARY CRITICISMS, furnishing impartial and thoughtful reviews of the leading productions of the press in all languages.

OUR MONTHLY GOSSIP, a department abounding in short and lively articles on persons of note, incidents of the day and other novel or amusing topics.

ILLUSTRATIONS, by artists and engravers of accomplished skill, profusely introduced, and constituting a most attractive feature.

TERMS.—Yearly Subscription, $4; Two Copies, $7; Five Copies, $16; Ten Copies, $30, with a copy gratis to the person procuring the club; Single Number, 35 cents. SPECIMEN NUMBER mailed, postage paid, to any address, on receipt of 20 cents.

BACK NUMBERS can always be supplied.

Address

J. B. LIPPINCOTT & CO., PUBLISHERS,

715 and 717 *MARKET ST., PHILADELPHIA*

INCORPORATED 1835.

1875.

OFFICE OF THE

DELAWARE MUTUAL SAFETY INSURANCE CO,

Philadelphia, November 10, 1875.

ASSETS OF THE COMPANY, November 1, 1875.

$150,000	United States Six Per Cent. Loan, 1897	$185,250 00
184,000	State of Pennsylvania Six Per Cent. Loans	205,540 00
325,000	City of Philadelphia " " " (exempt from tax)	350,575 00
250,000	State of New Jersey " " " 1880 to 1902	268,460 00
100,000	City of Pittsburgh Seven " "	107,000 00
100,000	City of Boston Six Per Cent. Loans	107,000 00
20,000	Pennsylvania Railroad First Mortgage Six Per Cent. Bonds	20,800 00
25,000	Western Penna. Railroad Mortgage " " " (Penna. Railroad Guarantee)	19,500 00
44,000	State of Tennessee Six Per Cent. Loan	20,680 00
19,000	Pennsylvania Railroad Company . 380 Shares Stock	19,380 00
6,050	North Pennsylvania Railroad Comp'y, 121 " "	6,413 00
5,000	Centennial Board of Finance . 500 " "	5,000 00
40,000	American Steamship Company Six Per Cent. Bonds	29,600 00
271,950	Loans on Bond and Mortgage, first liens on City Properties	271,950 00
$1,540,000	Par. Cost, $1,542,718.44 Market Value,	$1,617,148 00
	Real Estate at Philadelphia and Pittsburgh	120,000 00
	Bills Receivable for Insurances made	213,574 55
	Balances Due at Agencies,—Premiums on Marine Policies.	
	—Accrued Interest and other debts due the Company	67,113 28
	Stock and Scrip, etc., of Sundry Corporations, $17,043. Estimated value	6,789 00
	Cash—On deposit in Banks . $175,531 46	
	Loaned on call with collaterals . 120,000 00	
	In Office . 839 84	$296,371 30
		$2,320,996 13

DIRECTORS:

Thomas C. Hand,	John D. Taylor,	Jacob Riegel,
James Traquair,	George W. Bernadou,	Thomas P. Stotesbury,
Henry P. Sloan,	Wm. C. Houston,	Jacob P. Jones,
John H. Catherwood,	H. Frank Robinson,	James B. McFarland,
N. Parker Shortridge,	Samuel E. Stokes,	Spencer McIlvaine,
Andrew Wheeler,	William G. Boulton,	John H. Michener,
James C. Hand,	Edward Darlington,	A. B. Berger, Pittsburgh
William C. Ludwig,	H. Jones Brooke,	D. T. Morgan, "
Hugh Craig,	Edward Lafourcade,	Wm. S. Bissell, "

HENRY LYLBURN, Secretary.
HENRY BALL, Ass't Secretary.

THOMAS C. HAND, President.

STEPHEN F. WHITMAN & SON,
Specialties in Rare Confections
FOR CHOICE PRESENTS.

S. W. Cor. of Twelfth and Market Sts., Philadelphia.
BRANCH MANUFACTORY,
Machinery Hall, Exposition Grounds.

STRAWBRIDGE & CLOTHIER,

IMPORTERS,

And Wholesale and Retail Dealers in

DRY GOODS,

NORTHWEST CORNER

Eighth and Market Streets,

PHILADELPHIA,

respectfully invite the attention of strangers visiting our city during the Centennial year to their very extensive assortment of general Dry Goods, unsurpassed in any market of this country.

It being impossible to name all our various departments, we specify only

SILKS AND DRESS GOODS,
SHAWLS AND SUITS,
HOSIERY AND UNDERWEAR,
KID GLOVES, etc.,

of which our stock is immense in new, fresh, and desirable goods.

It is our intention to make use of the opportunity afforded by the Centennial year to show strangers and residents of other States that Philadelphia prices for Dry Goods are the lowest of any market of this country. More than ever before shall it be our constant effort to make every purchaser at our house a permanent customer. To this end we shall allow no goods to be sold over our counters but those of standard and reliable qualities, and the prices shall be absolutely the lowest at which goods of intrinsic value can be sold.

All our prices are fixed, and admit of no deviation in any instance.

Our business is so transacted that the most inexperienced buyer can be always sure of doing as well in our house as the most skillful purchaser can do anywhere.

www.ingramcontent.com/pod-product-compliance
Lightning Source LLC
Chambersburg PA
CBHW030347170426
43202CB00010B/1276